STECK-VAUGHN

Level 1

W9-CPE-940

POWER UP!
BUILDING READING STRENGTH

WORKOUT BOOK
Teacher's Edition

PROGRAM AUTHORS

Senior Author
Dr. Roger Farr

Co-Authors
Elizabeth Haydel, M.Ed.
Kimberly Munroe, M.Ed.

STECK-VAUGHN
A Harcourt Company

www.steck-vaughn.com

Acknowledgments

Editorial Director	Diane Schnell
Supervising Editor	Jody Cosson
Editor	Erin Roberson
Associate Editor	Kelly Stern
Director of Design	Scott Huber
Associate Director of Design	Joyce Spicer
Supervising Designer	Pam Heaney
Designer	Jessica Bristow
Production Manager	S. Mychael Ferris-Pacheco
Production Coordinator	Paula Schumann
Electronic Production Artist	Julia Miracle Hagaman
Senior Technical Advisor	Alan Klemp
Image Services Coordinator	Ted Krause
Media Researcher	Alyx Kellington
Marketing Manager	Patricia Colacino

Photography

T-13 ©Mary Kate Denny/PhotoEdit; p.16 ©Hulton Archive/Getty Images; p.18 ©Hulton Archive/Getty Images; p.19 ©CORBIS; p.20 ©Leonard de Selva/CORBIS; p.24c ©Eduardo Garcia/Getty Images; p.41a ©Scott Polar Research Institute; p.43 ©Hulton Archive/Getty Images; p.55 ©Richard Cummins/CORBIS; p.76 ©Bettmann/CORBIS; p.80 ©Duomo/CORBIS; p.100 ©PhotoEdit; p.102 Courtesy of the Bridgeport Public Library; p.104 Courtesy The Barnum Museum, Bridgeport, CT; p.118 Courtesy of U.S. Representative Charles Gonzalez.

Additional photography by Corbis Royalty Free, John Foxx, Getty Royalty Free, Park Street Photography, Steck-Vaughn Collection, and StockByte.

Illustrations

Pp.4, 7, 8 Mark Braught; pp.29, 31, 32 Janet Wilson; pp.64, 65, 66, 67 Linda Sturm; pp.88, 91 Gary Glover.

ISBN 0-7398-5082-2

Copyright © 2003 Steck-Vaughn Company

Power Up! Building Reading Strength is a trademark of Steck-Vaughn Company.

Printed in the United States of America.

4 5 6 7 8 9 WC 06 05 04 03 02

CONTENTS

Annotated Student Pages

Program Overview

PowerUp!™ *Building Reading Strength* is a comprehensive, leveled reading program designed to reach middle-school students who have yet to master the reading strategies and skills they need to make literacy progress. The program empowers struggling readers to experience success.

Power Up! provides teachers with everything they need to implement the program and with the flexibility to accommodate students' individual skill levels, learning styles, and experiences to ensure that no student is left behind.

Power Up! focuses on the same research-based strategies and skills in reading and writing as those identified in the *Standards for the English Language Arts* compiled by the International Reading Association (IRA) and the National Council of Teachers of English (NCTE). *Power Up!* provides the continued, systematic reading instruction called for by the IRA and the National Middle-School Association's (NMSA) joint position paper entitled *Supporting Young Adolescents' Literacy Learning.* The program aligns with reading language arts curriculum standards commonly implemented by states and districts and measured by all major standardized tests. This close alignment with standards, curricula, and assessments helps ensure that students receive instruction in the strategies and skills that they need most and in the same important areas as their classmates.

Power Up! can be used in a variety of settings. Some schools may use *Power Up!* as a whole-class intervention or remedial reading program, while other schools might use it as the instructional component of a literacy intervention pull-out program. In yet other schools, *Power Up!* might be used as a supplemental program for students who need additional instruction within a regular reading or language arts classroom. The breadth and depth of student materials and teacher support allow the program to be tailored to fit individual situations.

Program Levels

Power Up! Building Reading Strength is a four-level program. The student materials have been carefully developed within a designated range of reading levels to help ensure consistency in the readability of the materials and increase the likelihood of student success.

Power Up! Level	Level Icon	Harris-Jacobson Readability Range (Grade Level)
1		2.5 – 3.0
2		3.0 – 3.5
3		3.5 – 4.5
4		4.5 – 5.5

Program Components

Power Up! Building Reading Strength student materials are high-interest/low-readability *Paperback Books, Workout Books,* and technology (*Power Up! on the Web* and books on *Audio Cassettes* and *CD-ROMs*). *Posters* promote interest in the topics and titles students will read and guide students to use the reading strategies that all good readers use. Teachers can select the program components that best fit their students' needs and their own teaching styles. Extensive teacher materials supply additional activities for reinforcement or reteaching via various technologies. This *Workout Book Teacher's Edition* supports the student activities with guidance for introducing, teaching, and reinforcing each lesson's strategies and skills. Ideas for reteaching and for instructional extensions enable teachers to adapt activities to fit each student. The *Teacher's Resource Binder* guides the teacher through all facets of the program.

Components for Level 1

Think-Along™ Approach

Program author Dr. Roger Farr has incorporated the successful Think-Along approach as a key element in the *Power Up!* program. Think-Along icons embedded within the *Paperback Books* prompt students to answer questions that encourage them to think as they read. The Think-Along questions are provided in write-in boxes in the *Workout Book* and in masters in the *Teacher's Resource Binder*.

Meeting the Needs of the Struggling Reader

The breadth and depth of instructional strategies and activities in *Power Up!* allow teachers to accommodate a variety of readers. Each lesson presents multiple teaching/reteaching and reciprocal teaching opportunities as well as reinforcement activities for students who need them. Special tips for teachers appear under the heading "Meeting Individual Needs" throughout this *Workout Book Teacher's Edition*. The *Paperback Books* on *Audio Cassette* and *CD-ROM* provide models of fluency and are practical alternatives for students who need audio/visual assistance with their reading.

Meeting the Needs of the ESL Reader

Several features of *Power Up!* attend to ESL readers' needs. Controlled vocabulary and attention to idiomatic language help make comprehension more accessible to ESL students. Unfamiliar words are defined in footnotes in the *Workout Book* selections and in the nonfiction *Paperback Book* glossaries. In addition, unique ESL features in this *Workout Book Teacher's Edition* and the *Teacher's Resource Binder* call attention to language- and culture-related knowledge that will aid students' reading comprehension.

Assessment

A variety of assessment options provides teachers with the information they need to make decisions about individual and group instruction, and to track progress over time. Formal assessments as well as suggestions for informal, portfolio, and student self-assessment provide options for gathering information about student progress.

Themes

Themes commonly used in middle-school and character education are woven throughout the student materials to provide a rich context for learning. Powerful themes such as responsibility, relationships, and resolving conflicts help make content relevant and engaging to students.

Strategies and Skills

Instructional activities focus on essential reading strategies, word analysis skills, word identification strategies (phonics), and writing forms appropriate for students at each level of literacy development. Strategies and skills are carefully articulated so that there is a measured progression both within and across levels. The Scope and Sequence chart on page T-8 lists the strategies and skills taught at each level.

About the

Workout Book

The **Workout Book** is organized into two themes with two fiction and two nonfiction selections per theme. Each selection is supported by the following activity pages.

Themes set the scene for the book-related activities, eliciting students' prior knowledge and providing a basis for writing and discussion.

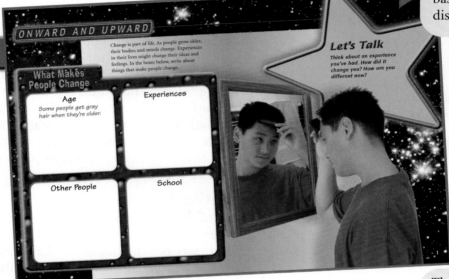

The **Vocabulary Builder** activity introduces the ten vocabulary words used in the selection.

The **Getting Ready to Read** activity explains the reading strategy being taught.

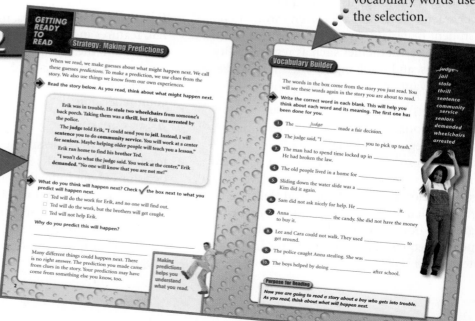

3

In the selection, which is the excerpted first chapter of the *Paperback Book*, **Think-Along** questions help students apply a specific reading strategy and think about their reading.

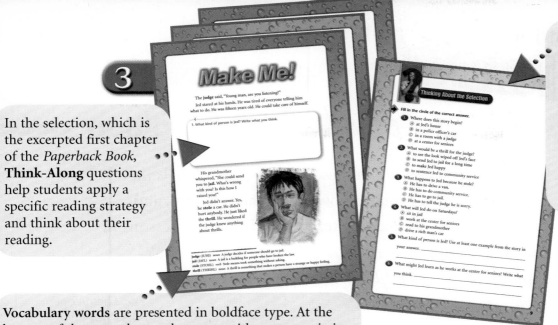

Thinking About the Selection assesses students' comprehension of what they have read and helps prepare them for taking standardized tests.

Vocabulary words are presented in boldface type. At the bottom of the page, the words appear with a pronunciation respelling, the part of speech in which the word is used in the selection, and a brief definition.

4

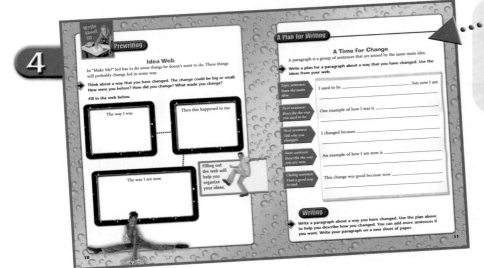

Write About It! leads students through a tightly guided writing process, from forming ideas to writing their final draft.

Words, Words, Words presents word analysis skills that every good reader needs to know.

5

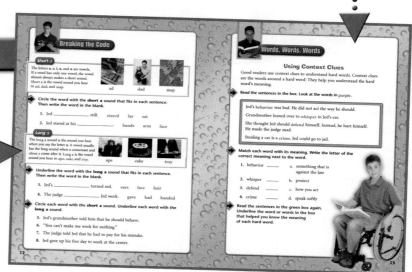

Breaking the Code introduces students to strategies for basic word identification.

Workout Book Teacher's Edition

The material presented in these teacher pages details the product purpose, explains how to use the program, and provides the novice reading teacher with valuable lessons in teaching reading. The material in the rest of this book supports the *Workout Book* in the following ways.

The **Theme** opener offers tips on introducing the theme and provides an overview of the skills and strategies presented in the theme.

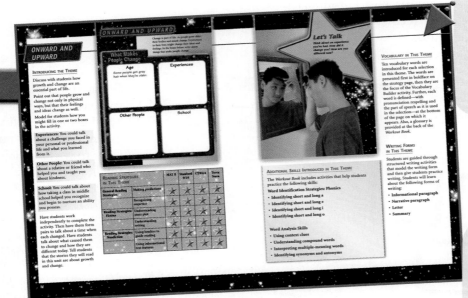

Getting Ready to Read offers further explanation of the reading strategy being taught and provides tips on introducing the strategy.

Vocabulary Builder provides answers to the activity, a vocabulary extension activity, and further assessment of students' comprehension of the vocabulary words.

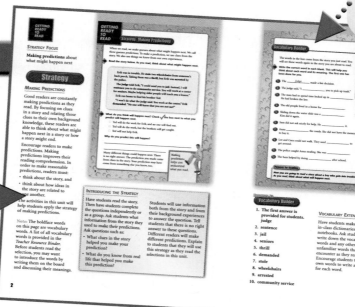

3

The selection support provides:
- interesting background material to share with students.
- tips for before, during, and after reading.
- models of student and teacher responses to the Think-Along questions and reteaching tips to help students respond to the Think-Along questions.
- tips for teaching the reading strategy.
- ideas for Meeting Individual Needs, assisting ESL learners, and integrating Reciprocal Teaching models.

Thinking About the Selection provides an answer key and information to share with students about testing situations. After students have read the selection, a list of similar books for further reading and an activity to promote family involvement are provided.

4

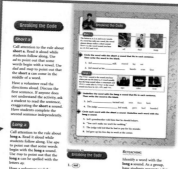

Write About It! offers tips to help students before, during, and after writing. A rubric for each writing form is provided at point of use for ease in scoring. Discussion and Group Sharing activities, along with Portfolio and Student Self-Assessment ideas, help students think about, share, and improve their writing.

5

Both **Breaking the Code** and **Words, Words, Words** offer step-by-step instructions on teaching the skill, an answer key for the activity, and a reteaching activity.

A Research-Based Program

POWER UP! was created to help middle-school students become successful readers by using an integrated instructional model based on more than thirty years of experience in reading research and the teaching of reading.

Power Up! Building Reading Strength was developed to help improve reading skills in middle school by addressing the needs of both students and teachers. According to Donahue, Voelkl, Campbell, and Mazzeo (1999), the 1998 National Assessment of Educational Progress (NAEP) results indicated that only 33% of eighth-grade students were reading at a proficient level and almost 25% were reading below a basic level. The issue of low reading proficiency is a critical matter because reading at the middle-school level involves an increased emphasis on more complex and less familiar expository texts, and is often a bellwether for predicting student success.

Under the leadership of Senior Author Dr. Roger Farr and his colleagues, *Power Up!* was created to help middle-school students become successful readers by using an integrated instructional model based on more than thirty years of experience in reading research and the teaching of reading. The program supports many of the conclusions reached by the Washington Department of Public Instruction (1998) and the National Reading Panel (2000) by combining a variety of research-evidenced instructional techniques into a single, comprehensive approach to teaching reading at the middle-school level.

Power Up! provides reading and content area teachers with a tool to focus on the reading needs of their students by using research-verified instructional pedagogies in critical reading skill areas, including:

(**1**) comprehension strategies;
(**2**) the transition from narrative to expository text;
(**3**) guided reading;
(**4**) vocabulary; and
(**5**) the connection between reading and writing.

These areas of study are supported using a variety of materials, including technology solutions. Instructional techniques include the use of systematic practice of new skills and scaffolded support.

Comprehension Strategies

Durkin (1993) viewed reading comprehension as essential not only to academic learning but to lifelong learning, defining it as "intentional thinking during which meaning is constructed through interactions between text and reader." *Power Up!* uses a multiple-strategy approach to reading comprehension that the National Reading Panel (2000) reports is empirically supported as "lead[ing] to increased learning of the strategies, to specific transfer of learning, to increased retention, and [the] understanding of new passages." Among the research techniques supported by the program are thinking aloud [Think-Alongs] (Baumann, Seifert-Kessell, and Jones, 1992; Davey, 1983; and Loxterman, Beck, and McKeown, 1994); metacognitive and comprehension monitoring (Katims and Harris, 1997; Tregaskes and Daines, 1989; and Taylor and Frye, 1992); and reciprocal teaching (Palincsar and Brown, 1984; and Lysynchuk, Pressley, and Vye, 1990).

Transition from Narrative to Expository Texts

Students are increasingly expected to process text that conveys information as its primary function. *Power Up!* uses leveled, complementary narrative and expository texts as a scaffold to using the informational texts that will form the primary foundation for students' future studies and eventually their work lives. This approach embraces the National Reading Panel (2000) assertion that encourages "the importance of using a wide variety of print throughout the curriculum, including high-quality children's/adolescents' literature and diverse expository materials appropriate to the age and developmental level of learners." It also promotes the use of research-based expository text instruction and strategies to improve reading success (Carnine and Kinder, 1985; Dole, Valencia, Greer, and Wardrop, 1991; Franklin, Roach, and Clary, 1992; Stevens, 1988; and Taylor and Beach, 1984).

Guided Reading

According to the National Reading Panel (2000), "teacher educators, educational researchers and theorists have called for more attention to direct instruction in fluency." Research indicates that guided reading and other fluency-related procedures in which students read passages multiple times while receiving guidance or feedback are effective in improving a variety of reading skills. Snow, Burns, and Griffin (1998) stated that "adequate progress in learning to read English (or any alphabetic language) beyond the initial level depends on sufficient practice in reading to achieve fluency with different texts." Research points out that only through extended reading practice do students develop fluency skills that go beyond accuracy of recognition to automaticity of recognition (Allington, 1984; and Snow et al., 1998). *Power Up!* provides numerous opportunities for teachers to employ guided and shared reading, oral reading feedback, or reading while listening.

Vocabulary

In its review of scientifically based research in the area of vocabulary as it relates to reading development, the National Reading Panel (2000) concluded that "vocabulary instruction should be incorporated into reading instruction." Among the instructional findings suggested by the National Reading Panel (2000) and supported by *Power Up!* are that:
(1) vocabulary should be taught both directly and indirectly;
(2) repetition and multiple exposures to vocabulary items are important;
(3) learning in rich contexts is valuable for vocabulary learning;
(4) vocabulary learning should be an active experience; and
(5) dependence on a single vocabulary instruction method will not result in optimal learning.

The Connection Between Reading and Writing

The relationship between reading and writing is well established in the research literature on reading achievement (Squire, 1983; and Tierney and Shanahan, 1991). *Power Up!* reinforces reading development by using writing as a tool to encourage comprehension and extend learning.

Senior Author Dr. Roger Farr

Dr. Roger Farr is Chancellor's Professor Emeritus at Indiana University. Since 1985 he has been Associate Director of the Center for Innovation in Assessment, the hub of his extensive research and development activities. He served for ten years as the Associate Director of the ERIC Clearinghouse on Reading, English, and Communication. Dr. Farr earned his Ed.D. in Reading and Educational Psychology at the State University of New York. In addition to having taught elementary school through graduate school, Dr. Farr has authored several assessments. Among the standardized tests he has participated in developing are the *Iowa Silent Reading Tests* and the *Metropolitan Achievement Tests* (MAT). Dr. Farr has been the author of educational programs used to teach millions of students at all levels, including having served with Dr. Dorothy Strickland as co-senior author of the Harcourt Reading series. Dr. Farr was co-editor of the *Reading Research Quarterly*, the world's leading research journal in the field of language education, for 11 years. He has served with distinction in numerous professional organizations, most notably as president of the International Reading Association (IRA).

Dr. Farr has long been a leading authority on the assessment of language usage and reading. For more than thirty years, his ongoing research has directed his development of outstanding assessment instruments and instructional approaches. The national recognition of his work led to Dr. Farr's appointment as a special consultant to the National Assessment of Educational Progress (NAEP). In recognition of the direct connection between his valuable research and excellent teaching, the IRA honored Dr. Farr in 1984 with the William S. Gray Citation of Merit for Outstanding Lifetime Contributions to the Teaching of Reading. In 1987, IRA named him its Outstanding Teacher Educator in Reading.

Scope and Sequence

Strategy / Skill	Level 1	Level 2	Level 3	Level 4
GENERAL READING STRATEGIES				
Making Predictions	✓		✓	
Recognizing Sequence	✓		✓	
Identifying Main Idea and Details	✓		✓	
Identifying Facts and Opinions	✓		✓	
Comparing and Contrasting		✓		✓
Identifying Cause and Effect		✓		✓
Making Inferences/Drawing Conclusions		✓		✓
Recognizing Author's Viewpoint and Purpose		✓		✓
READING STRATEGIES: NONFICTION				
Using headers and subheaders to guide reading	•	•	✓	✓
Using informational text features (including table of contents, index, and glossary)	•	•	✓	✓
Interpreting pictures, graphs, and charts	•	•	✓	✓
Using research skills and strategies to extend a topic	•	•	✓	✓
READING STRATEGIES: FICTION				
Story Plot	•	•	✓	✓
Setting	•	•	✓	✓
Character	•	•	✓	✓
Theme	•	•	✓	✓
WRITING FORMS				
Informational Essays	✓	✓	✓	✓
Narratives (stories, real or imagined)	✓	✓	✓	✓
Letters	✓	✓	✓	✓
Summaries	✓	✓	✓	✓
Instructions	✓	✓	✓	✓
Reviews	✓	✓	✓	✓
Persuasive Essays	✓	✓	✓	✓
Speeches	✓	✓	✓	✓

✓ = introduced/taught in the *Workout Book*
• = introduced in the *Workout Book Teacher's Edition*

Strategy / Skill	Level 1	Level 2	Level 3	Level 4
WORD IDENTIFICATION STRATEGIES: PHONICS				
Short and long *a*	✓			
Short and long *e*	✓			
Short and long *i*	✓			
Short and long *o*	✓			
Short and long *u*	✓			
Variant consonants – *g*	✓			
Variant consonants – *c*	✓			
Variant consonants – *s*	✓			
Initial, medial, and final consonant digraphs – *ph, gh*		✓		
R-controlled vowels – *er, ir, ur*		✓		
R-controlled vowels – *ar, or*		✓		
Vowel digraph – *oo*		✓		
Sounds of *ow*		✓		
Sounds of *ou*		✓		
Dipthongs – *oi, oy*		✓		
Silent consonants – *kn, wr, gh*		✓		
WORD ANALYSIS				
Using context clues	✓	✓	✓	✓
Understanding compound words	✓	✓	✓	✓
Interpreting multiple-meaning words	✓	✓	✓	✓
Identifying synonyms and antonyms	✓	✓	✓	✓
Understanding/using homonyms, homographs, and homophones	✓	✓	✓	✓
Using prefixes, suffixes, and roots of words	✓	✓	✓	✓
Interpreting figurative language (including similes and metaphors)	✓	✓	✓	✓
Using reference materials (including dictionary and thesaurus)	✓	✓	✓	✓

Correlations to the Standards

Power Up! Building Reading Strength encompasses the curriculum objectives that most states and districts require and that most standardized tests measure, as shown in the chart on the facing page. Additionally, the International Reading Association (IRA) and the National Council of Teachers of English (NCTE) have jointly prepared the *Standards for the English Language Arts. Power Up!* meets the following standards:

▶ Students read a wide range of print texts, including fiction and nonfiction.

▶ Students read a wide range of literature from many genres.

▶ Students use their prior knowledge, interact with other readers and writers, use word identification strategies, and use their understanding of text features, such as sound-letter correspondence and context, to comprehend, interpret, evaluate, and appreciate texts.

▶ Students learn to communicate effectively with a variety of audiences in spoken and written language by using appropriate vocabulary, conventions, and style.

▶ Students use different elements of the writing process to communicate effectively with a variety of audiences.

▶ Students accomplish life purposes by using spoken, written, and visual language.

Furthermore, the IRA has joined with the National Middle School Association (NMSA) to request that a greater priority be placed on reading instruction at the middle-school level. The associations have recommended the following actions:

▶ continuous reading instruction for all middle-school students;

▶ reading instruction that is appropriate for individual learners;

▶ assessment measures that inform instruction, showing learners their strengths as well as their needs; and

▶ opportunities for students to read and to discuss reading with others.

To meet these goals, IRA and NMSA have requested that:

▶ a wide variety of print and nonprint resources be made available to students;

▶ teachers and other professionals model good reading habits and strategies for students;

▶ a variety of text types be made available for students; and

▶ students be encouraged to read.

Power Up! Building Reading Strength meets the needs of struggling middle-school readers in areas that IRA, NMSA, and NCTE have outlined.

How *Power Up!* Correlates to Standardized Tests and National Standards

Power Up! Strategy / Skill	MAT 8[1]	SAT 10[2]	CTB Writing Assessment[3]	Terra Nova[4]	NAEP[5]	National Standards[6]	MCREL[7]
GENERAL READING STRATEGIES							
Making Predictions	✓	✓	•	✓	✓	✓	✓
Identifying Main Idea and Details	✓	✓	•	✓	✓	✓	✓
Identifying Facts and Opinions	✓	✓	•	✓	✓	✓	✓
Recognizing Sequence	✓	✓	•	✓	✓	✓	✓
Comparing and Contrasting	✓	✓	•	✓	✓	✓	✓
Identifying Cause and Effect	✓	✓	•	✓	✓	✓	✓
Making Inferences/Drawing Conclusions	✓	✓	•	✓	✓	✓	✓
Recognizing Author's Viewpoint and Purpose	✓	✓	•	✓	✓	✓	✓
WRITING FORMS							
Informational Essays	✓	✓	✓	•	✓	✓	✓
Narratives	✓	✓	✓	•	✓	✓	✓
Summaries			✓	•		✓	✓
Letters				•			✓
Reviews		✓		•			✓
Persuasive Essays		✓	✓	•	✓	✓	✓
Speeches				•			
Instructions				•			✓

✓ = Appears at several test levels or grade levels including grades 6–8

• = Assessment does not test these skills

[1] Metropolitan Achievement Test, 8th Edition, Harcourt Educational Measurement
[2] Stanford Achievement Test, 10th Edition, Harcourt Educational Measurement
[3] CTB Writing Assessment, California Test Bureau: McGraw-Hill
[4] Terra Nova, 2nd Edition, California Test Bureau: McGraw-Hill
[5] National Assessment of Educational Progress. Note: NAEP has organized the reading frameworks around four different stances for comprehension.
[6] New Standards Assessment, Harcourt Educational Measurement
[7] Mid-Continent Research for Education and Learning, Aurora, Colorado. MCREL reviewed the standards for 49 states and developed a compendium of language arts standards.

Common Reading Terms

Cognition is the act of using one's thought processes to construct meaning. Cognition is an active process in which a learner takes in new information and relates it to what is already known. Cognition in reading is the active process of making sense of an author's ideas and relating those ideas to our own.

Graphic Organizers are a means of visually representing a set of related ideas and are often used to help students develop ideas for writing. Graphic organizers include flowcharts, timelines, webs, visual maps, and Venn diagrams. Many language arts writing assessments encourage students to use a graphic organizer as an aid in planning their writing.

Metacognition is the act of understanding how one understands or knows. While cognition is the actual act of understanding, metacognition is the understanding of the active processes a learner engages in order to understand. Many theorists and practitioners who have studied metacognition propose three basic aspects:

▶ *First, one needs to develop a plan of action.* Ask yourself, "Why am I reading this selection and what should I do first?"

▶ *Second, one needs to maintain/monitor the plan.* Ask yourself, "Am I accomplishing my purpose and what can I do if I am not meeting my goals?"

▶ *Third, one needs to evaluate how well the plan was accomplished.* Ask yourself, "Did I achieve all that I could have and can I apply this approach to other reading tasks?"

Phonics is often thought to be a method of reading instruction that is based on the sound/symbol relationships in language. Phonics, however, is not a method of instruction. Rather, it is an understanding of the connection between spoken and written sounds.

Reading Strategies are processes that a reader employs, either consciously or unconsciously, to make meaning of a text. Reading comprehension strategies include both cognitive and metacognitive strategies. Cognitive strategies include such activities as making predictions, connecting the text to other texts and other experiences, summarizing, and visualizing. Metacognitive strategies include awareness and control of such strategies as knowing when to re-read or adjust the pace of reading.

Reciprocal Teaching (Palincsar, 1986) is an instructional approach that helps students think about and use reading strategies. When using reciprocal teaching, the teacher and students take turns generating questions about and summaries of passages of text. They stop at various places in a text, summarize what they have read, ask questions about the text, clarify parts of the text that were confusing, and predict what the text will be about next.

Rubrics are specific statements of progressive levels of achievement. In writing assessment, rubrics are statements that provide students and teachers with specific information about what good writing should include.

Schema is the organization structure we have for various concepts. A reader or listener organizes information by relating it to a schema. We each have a schema for the concept of fishing, for example. We expect to hear about fishing equipment, types of fish, etc. A schema is, therefore, a set of related place-holders that can be filled in by context or additional information from text, audio or visual media, or a speaker.

Standards are statements of expected learning outcomes. Standards are developed to be specific enough so that teachers, parents, and students know exactly what is required. Standards are often written so that assessments can be easily developed.

Thinking Along is the cognitive process of reading. Every reading event can be a Think-Along activity. The reader should be thinking along as he or she is reading.

Think-Aloud is a Think-Along that is verbalized. If a reader says aloud what he or she is thinking as he or she reads, the reader is doing a think-aloud. Teachers demonstrate the cognitive process of reading by thinking. The person doing the think-aloud is not necessarily suggesting that what he or she is thinking is what the listener should be thinking. The goal is to develop in each reader the process of Thinking Along with a text.

Word Analysis is the act of analyzing a word to determine its meaning and pronunciation. Word analysis includes the study of word parts, compound words, phonics (sound/symbol relations), syllabication, and the use of context clues.

Tips for Teaching Reading

Below are some tips for teaching reading that research has shown promote literacy development.

Before Reading

▶ Activate students' schema (background knowledge) by engaging them in discussion and writing on the topic of the reading selection.

▶ Introduce the selection and encourage students to discuss, question, and predict.

During Reading

▶ Think aloud by reading aloud and modeling your thought processes.

▶ Promote buddy reading, in which students take turns reading every other page or paragraph with a partner.

▶ Encourage students to write about what they are reading.

▶ Observe students during reading to assess comprehension.

▶ Ask students to share their questions and thoughts as they read.

▶ Assess struggling students by using running records to determine their word recognition skills.

After Reading

▶ Provide opportunities for students to write about what they have read.

▶ Ask students to summarize and retell what they have read.

▶ Encourage students to think about and discuss their reading strategies.

As Part of All Classroom Instruction

▶ Read to students every day, modeling your own fluent reading.

▶ Have students read and write independently every day.

▶ Provide opportunities for students to participate in cooperative learning groups.

▶ Keep a small in-class library of level-appropriate, high-interest magazines and fiction and nonfiction books available for students to read.

▶ Vary instructional activities to reach students who have different learning styles.

▶ On a regular basis, collect information about each student's reading skills and strategies.

Additional Tips for Reading Teachers

▶ Try to teach word recognition skills, including phonics and vocabulary, as opportunities to use those skills are presented in the stories and selections students are reading.

▶ Provide opportunities for students to see how the reading skills and strategies they are learning apply across the content areas by modeling the skills and strategies using content-area materials.

▶ Praise and encourage your students for reading.

▶ Use word play to engage students in phonemic awareness and phonics activities (including rhymes, tongue twisters, and shared stories or poems).

▶ Look for, make note of, and try new ideas for effectively teaching reading.

Using Think-Along Questions in the Classroom

Before beginning the *Power Up!* program, you might want to model for students the reading strategies that they use while they read. Having this example will help students to understand that even good readers do not comprehend automatically just by looking at the words on the page. Good readers connect with and think about the text as they read.

To model thinking along for students:

▶ choose a text with which you are familiar;

▶ provide students with copies of the text so they can follow along;

▶ read the text aloud, stopping to share your thoughts every five or six sentences; and

▶ share your thoughts when you are predicting, visualizing, comparing, or using other comprehension strategies.

We know that students will learn when they are presented with opportunities to practice newly acquired skills and time to reflect on their performance. The Think-Along questions in the *Workout Books* and activities in this *Workout Book Teacher's Edition* will provide students with opportunities for practice and reflection. You can also use the Think-Along process with other texts.

To do so, you can:

▶ read texts aloud and pause at appropriate places to ask questions, such as *What do you think will happen next?* or *What does this remind you of?*

▶ add your own Think-Along questions to computer-generated texts.

▶ have students use light pencil marks or sticky notes to mark stopping points in other books they are reading.

When students have responded to their reading, you can ask questions such as:

▶ *That's an interesting idea. What made you think that?*

▶ *I like that idea. Where did it come from?*

▶ *I think I know what you mean. Can you respond a little more?*

▶ *I never thought of that. What made you think of that?*

These kinds of questions will help students reflect on what they have read.

Research has shown that it is important to be explicit in the teaching of reading skills and strategies. Modeling your own strategy use and then providing students with the chance for practice and reflection will help them be strategic and comprehending readers.

ONWARD AND UPWARD

INTRODUCING THE THEME

Discuss with students how growth and change are an essential part of life.

Point out that people grow and change not only in physical ways, but that their feelings and ideas change as well.

Model for students how you might fill in one or two boxes in the activity.

Experiences: You could talk about a challenge you faced in your personal or professional life and what you learned from it.

Other People: You could talk about a relative or friend who helped you and taught you about kindness.

School: You could talk about how taking a class in middle school helped you recognize and begin to nurture an ability you possess.

Have students work independently to complete the activity. Then have them form pairs to talk about a time when each changed. Have students talk about what caused them to change and how they are different today. Tell students that the stories they will read in this unit are about growth and change.

Change is part of life. As people grow older, their bodies and minds change. Experiences in their lives might change their ideas and feelings. In the boxes below, write about things that make people change.

What Makes People Change

Age
Some people get gray hair when they're older.

Experiences

Other People

School

READING STRATEGIES IN THIS THEME		MAT 8	Stanford 9/10	CTBS/4	Terra Nova
General Reading Strategies	**Making predictions**	★	★	★	★
	Recognizing sequence	★	★	★	★
Reading Strategies: *Fiction*	**Understanding story plot**	★	★	★	★
	Understanding setting	★	★	★	★
Reading Strategies: *Nonfiction*	**Using headers to guide reading**	★	★	★	★
	Using informational text features	★	★	★	★

Let's Talk

Think about an experience you've had. How did it change you? How are you different now?

VOCABULARY IN THIS THEME

Ten vocabulary words are introduced for each selection in this theme. The words are presented first in boldface on the strategy page, then they are the focus of the Vocabulary Builder activity. Further, each word is defined—with pronunciation respelling and the part of speech as it is used in the selection—at the bottom of the page on which it appears. Also, a glossary is provided at the back of the *Workout Book.*

WRITING FORMS IN THIS THEME

Students are guided through structured writing activities that model the writing form and then give students practice writing. Students will learn about the following forms of writing:

- **Informational paragraph**
- **Narrative paragraph**
- **Letter**
- **Summary**

ADDITIONAL SKILLS INTRODUCED IN THIS THEME

The *Workout Book* includes activities that help students practice the following skills:

Word Identification Strategies: Phonics

- **Identifying short and long a**
- **Identifying short and long e**
- **Identifying short and long i**
- **Identifying short and long o**

Word Analysis Skills

- **Using context clues**
- **Understanding compound words**
- **Interpreting multiple-meaning words**
- **Identifying synonyms and antonyms**

STRATEGY FOCUS

Making predictions about what might happen next

Strategy

MAKING PREDICTIONS

Good readers are constantly making predictions as they read. By focusing on clues in a story and relating those clues to their own background knowledge, these readers are able to think about what might happen next in a story or how a story might end.

Encourage readers to make predictions. Making predictions improves their reading comprehension. In order to make reasonable predictions, readers must:

- think about the story, and
- think about how ideas in the story are related to one another.

The activities in this unit will help students apply the strategy of making predictions.

Note: The boldface words on this page are vocabulary words. A list of all vocabulary words is provided in the *Teacher's Resource Binder.* Before students read the selection, you may want to introduce the words by writing them on the board and discussing their meanings.

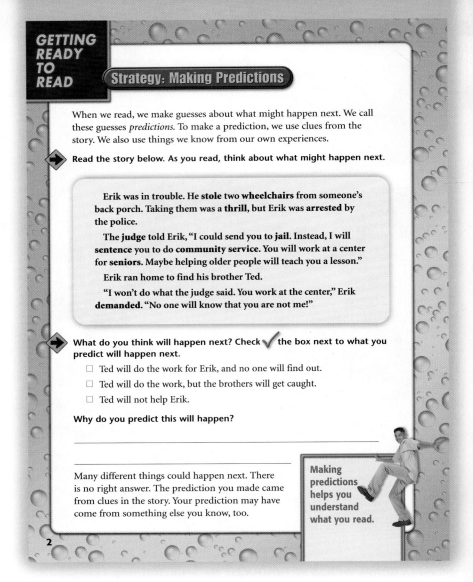

GETTING READY TO READ

Strategy: Making Predictions

When we read, we make guesses about what might happen next. We call these guesses *predictions.* To make a prediction, we use clues from the story. We also use things we know from our own experiences.

➡ **Read the story below. As you read, think about what might happen next.**

Erik was in trouble. He **stole** two **wheelchairs** from someone's back porch. Taking them was a **thrill,** but Erik was **arrested** by the police.

The **judge** told Erik, "I could send you to **jail.** Instead, I will **sentence** you to do **community service.** You will work at a center for **seniors.** Maybe helping older people will teach you a lesson."

Erik ran home to find his brother Ted.

"I won't do what the judge said. You work at the center," Erik **demanded.** "No one will know that you are not me!"

➡ **What do you think will happen next? Check ✓ the box next to what you predict will happen next.**

☐ Ted will do the work for Erik, and no one will find out.

☐ Ted will do the work, but the brothers will get caught.

☐ Ted will not help Erik.

Why do you predict this will happen?

_____

_____

Many different things could happen next. There is no right answer. The prediction you made came from clues in the story. Your prediction may have come from something else you know, too.

Making predictions helps you understand what you read.

2

INTRODUCING THE STRATEGY

Have students read the story. Then have students complete the questions independently or as a group. Ask students what information from the story they used to make their predictions. Ask questions such as:

- What clues in the story helped you make your prediction?

- What do you know from real life that helped you make this prediction?

Students will use information both from the story and from their background experiences to answer the question. Tell students that there is no right answer to these questions. Different readers will make different predictions. Explain to students that they will use this strategy as they read the selections in this unit.

The words in the box come from the story you just read. You will see these words again in the story you are about to read.

judge
jail
stole
thrill
sentence
community service
seniors
demanded
wheelchairs
arrested

Write the correct word in each blank. This will help you think about each word and its meaning. The first one has been done for you.

1. The _____judge_____ made a fair decision.

2. The judge said, "I _____ you to pick up trash."

3. The man had to spend time locked up in _____. He had broken the law.

4. The old people lived in a home for _____.

5. Sliding down the water slide was a _____. Kim did it again.

6. Sam did not ask nicely for help. He _____ it.

7. Anna _____ the candy. She did not have the money to buy it.

8. Lee and Cara could not walk. They used _____ to get around.

9. The police caught Anna stealing. She was _____.

10. The boys helped by doing _____ after school.

Purpose for Reading

Now you are going to read a story about a boy who gets into trouble. As you read, think about what will happen next.

3

Answers to Vocabulary Builder

1. **The first answer is provided for students.** judge

2. **sentence**

3. **jail**

4. **seniors**

5. **thrill**

6. **demanded**

7. **stole**

8. **wheelchairs**

9. **arrested**

10. **community service**

VOCABULARY EXTENSION

Have students make their own in-class dictionaries in their notebooks. Ask students to write down the vocabulary words and any other unfamiliar words that they encounter as they read. Encourage students to use their own words to write a definition for each word.

Vocabulary Builder

Students are introduced to words from the story that might not be familiar to them and that are critical to understanding the story.

The activity prepares students to recognize and understand these words in the story. Also, these vocabulary words are defined in footnotes throughout the story.

Assessment

To check comprehension of the vocabulary words, have students write ten sentences, one for each word. Remind students that each sentence must show the meaning of the word.

- **arrested**
- **community service**
- **demanded**
- **jail**
- **judge**
- **seniors**
- **sentence**
- **stole**
- **thrill**
- **wheelchairs**

Make Me!

SELECTION AT A GLANCE

In this story, a boy named Jed is sentenced to work at a center for seniors after he is caught stealing a car. Jed is unhappy about having to do work for which he will not get paid.

INTERESTING FACTS

Explain that many young people volunteer in centers for seniors. They also work in soup kitchens, after-school tutoring programs, or animal shelters.

Another popular program is the Junior Red Cross. In fact, young people under age 24 make up 40 percent of all Red Cross volunteers.

Make Me!

The **judge** said, "Young man, are you listening?"

Jed stared at his hands. He was tired of everyone telling him what to do. He was fifteen years old. He could take care of himself.

> 1. What kind of person is Jed? Write what you think.

His grandmother whispered, "She could send you to **jail**. What's wrong with you? Is this how I raised you?"

Jed didn't answer. Yes, he **stole** a car. He didn't hurt anybody. He just liked the **thrill**. He wondered if the judge knew anything about thrills.

---

judge (JUHJ) *noun* A judge decides if someone should go to jail.
jail (JAYL) *noun* A jail is a building for people who have broken the law.
stole (STOHL) *verb* Stole means took something without asking.
thrill (THRIHL) *noun* A thrill is something that makes a person have a strange or happy feeling.

4

Before Reading

INTRODUCING THE SELECTION

Draw a two-column chart on the board. Tell students that in this story, a boy named Jed is punished for stealing a car. Ask students to predict what Jed's punishment will be. Write their predictions in the left column. Then ask students to predict how Jed will react to each punishment. Write these predictions in the right column. As they read, have students check their predictions.

During Reading

PURPOSE FOR READING

Students read to make predictions about how Jed will react to his punishment.

APPLYING THE STRATEGY

Have students read the story in the *Workout Book*. Explain that they are to answer the questions in the boxes as they read the story. Remind them that answering these questions will help them think about what is going to happen next.

Possible Responses

Question 1

He probably gets in trouble a lot.

The student draws a conclusion about the kind of person Jed is, based on information he or she has just read.

He's mean.

This brief response would benefit from elaboration. **Ask,** *Why do you think Jed is mean? How else would you describe Jed?*

"Jed, I could lock you away. It would give me a thrill to see that look wiped off your face," the judge said.

Jed looked up, but not because he was worried about going to jail. He was surprised that the judge used the word thrill just as he was thinking that word. It was strange. He looked at the judge. Was she a mind reader?

The judge threw up her hands. "Fine. Jed Wilson, I **sentence** you to sixty hours of **community service**. It must be done within three months."

2. How do you think Jed will feel about doing community service?

Jed's face turned red. The judge said, "You will work at a center for **seniors** for the next ten Saturdays. Maybe you'll learn something by helping older people." Jed couldn't believe it. The judge wanted him to work on Saturdays for nothing.

His grandmother whispered, "Say something!"

Jed looked at the judge. "What do I have to do there?" he **demanded**.

---

sentence (SEHNT ns) *verb* To sentence means to make someone who broke the law spend time in jail or do some work.
community service (kuh MYOO nuh tee SUR vihs) *noun* Community service is work that helps someone. People who have broken the law sometimes do this work. They do not get paid.
seniors (SEEN yuhrz) *noun* Seniors are older people.
demanded (dee MAND ehd) *verb* Demanded means asked for something but not in a nice way.

5

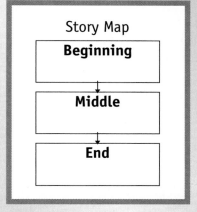

Strategy Tip

As students read, encourage them to think about what the people in the story might say or do next. Doing so will help them to better understand the story.

FICTION READING STRATEGY

Story Plot

Explain that plot is what happens in a story. It includes events that link together to form the story.

Story Map

Beginning
Middle
End

Have students complete a story map for this story. In the first box, have them describe the opening action of the story. In the second and third boxes, have them describe the main events in the middle and end of the story. Then have volunteers share their responses. Choose other stories that your students know, and ask them to identify the main events that make up the beginning, middle, and end.

Question 2

My uncle's car was stolen last summer.

While this student is relating the story to personal experiences, no prediction has been made. Encourage the student to predict how Jed will react to his sentence. **Say,** *You were thinking about something in your own life that relates to the story. How do you predict Jed will react to his punishment?*

He won't like it at all. If I were the judge I would have sent him to jail. He has a bad attitude!

This response indicates a good understanding of the story and of Jed's character. The student has responded to the question by drawing on the text and is providing a thoughtful opinion based on ideas in the text.

If students are having difficulty making predictions, model the process for them. **Say,** *When I predict, I use what I have read or clues from the pictures to help me figure out what will happen in the story. In this story, I am paying attention to what Jed says and does to make predictions about how he will react to his punishment.*

"The center is a place where seniors live. Sometimes older people need help. Sometimes they just don't want to live alone. Your job will be to do whatever they need."

---

3. What do you think the judge wants Jed to learn?

Jed stared at the floor. "No pay? No way," he said to himself.

The judge asked, "What did you say?"

"You can't make me work for nothing," Jed answered.

The judge lowered her voice. "Did you say I can't make you?" She shook her head and laughed.

Jed hated to be laughed at. His face got even redder. "Make me," he said.

The judge said, "Okay, I will."

His grandmother started crying. The judge started talking. That's how Jed started working at the center for seniors.

---

4. How might Jed feel on his first day at the center?

Possible Responses

Question 3

How hard it is to get old.

This response seems to indicate a lack of comprehension. However, it is possible that the student understood the story and is drawing on prior knowledge that reasonably leads to this conclusion. Encourage the student to explain how he or she arrived at this conclusion. **Say,** *What made you think this?*

Jed won't learn anything from the seniors.

This student has made a prediction. However, this response does not directly answer the question. **Ask,** *What do you think the judge wants Jed to learn from the seniors?*

Every Saturday, a police officer picked Jed up at his house. He drove Jed to work. The police officer always said the same thing. "Where to, work or jail?"

"Jail," Jed would whisper, and the officer would drive him to work.

Fifty seniors lived at the center. Some rode around in **wheelchairs.** Many took forever to walk down the hall. Jed hated the way everyone bossed him around. Someone was always asking for a drink of water. Others wanted him to find their glasses.

Some people wanted Jed to read letters to them. Jed really wanted to change the letters as he read them aloud. He wanted to fill them with scary stories, but he thought that the judge might find out. She would send him to jail, and that would upset his grandmother. He didn't like to make her worry. So he just read the letters the way they were written.

He hated his job.

---

wheelchairs (WEEL chehrz) *noun* Wheelchairs are chairs on wheels. These chairs are used by people who cannot walk.

7

Help students understand the meanings of idioms and multiple-meaning words, such as *look wiped off your face, he used to make fun of me,* or *if you don't mind.* Have students generate a list of different meanings of these words or idioms on the board. Then have the group write a sentence for each different meaning.

RECIPROCAL TEACHING

Summarize

Have students summarize what they read in the story. Start by telling them the main idea of the first part of the story. Tell them that a summary should include the main points; it does not have to include all the story details.

Write on the board, "A boy named Jed stole a car. He is sentenced to do community service. He will work at a center for seniors. Then . . ." Have students complete your summary by describing more main ideas in the order in which they occurred in the story. Students can do this individually or in pairs.

Question 4

Not good.

This student needs to elaborate on this response to make his or her thoughts more explicit. Encourage the student to tell more about how Jed will feel. **Say,** *Explain in what ways Jed will not feel good on his first day at the center.*

He will feel mad. He will not want to be there if he's not getting paid.

This response makes a valid prediction that reflects an accurate reading of the story. Encourage such responses.

After Reading

It is very important to have students read and discuss the predictions they have written in the boxes.

DISCUSSING THE RESPONSES

- Give as many students as possible a chance to tell what they wrote in one of the boxes.
- Have students explain what they were thinking when they wrote.
- Ask students how making predictions helped them think about the story.

RETEACHING

If students are having trouble responding to the questions in the boxes, **say,** *There are no right answers to the questions in the boxes. Write down what you are thinking in response to each question.*

Then model for them what you might have been thinking in response to the third question in the story. **Say,** *I was thinking that the judge wanted Jed to learn to be more responsible. I think the judge thinks that the older people will be good role models for Jed.*

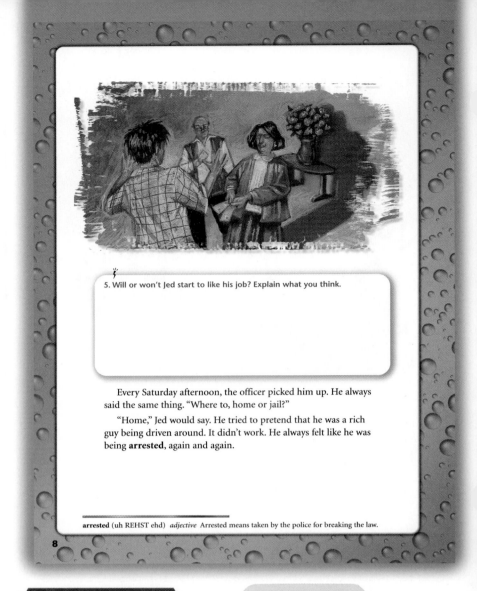

5. Will or won't Jed start to like his job? Explain what you think.

Every Saturday afternoon, the officer picked him up. He always said the same thing. "Where to, home or jail?"

"Home," Jed would say. He tried to pretend that he was a rich guy being driven around. It didn't work. He always felt like he was being **arrested**, again and again.

arrested (uh REHST ehd) *adjective* Arrested means taken by the police for breaking the law.

8

Assessment

Informal Assessment
To assess students' comprehension of the story, use their responses in the boxes and their discussion of their responses.

Student Self-Assessment
Encourage students to think about their reading experience by responding to this question: *How did answering the questions in the boxes help you think about what you were reading?*

Possible Responses

Question 5

Jed won't unless everyone stops bossing him around.

This student draws a logical conclusion. The student is relying on a detail in the text to support his or her response. Ask the student to make a prediction about what will happen in the story. **Say,** *Do you think that will happen?*

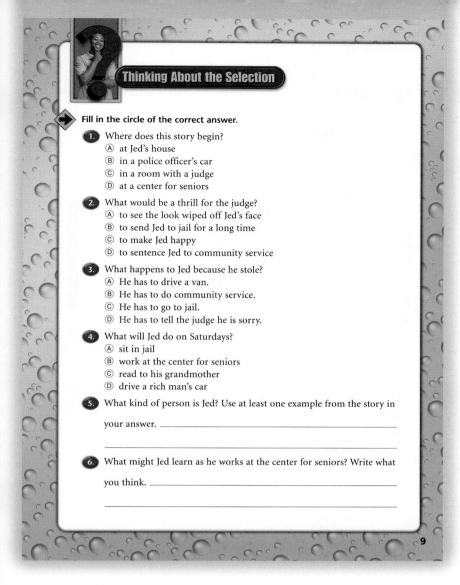

Fill in the circle of the correct answer.

1. Where does this story begin?
    Ⓐ at Jed's house
    Ⓑ in a police officer's car
    Ⓒ in a room with a judge
    Ⓓ at a center for seniors

2. What would be a thrill for the judge?
    Ⓐ to see the look wiped off Jed's face
    Ⓑ to send Jed to jail for a long time
    Ⓒ to make Jed happy
    Ⓓ to sentence Jed to community service

3. What happens to Jed because he stole?
    Ⓐ He has to drive a van.
    Ⓑ He has to do community service.
    Ⓒ He has to go to jail.
    Ⓓ He has to tell the judge he is sorry.

4. What will Jed do on Saturdays?
    Ⓐ sit in jail
    Ⓑ work at the center for seniors
    Ⓒ read to his grandmother
    Ⓓ drive a rich man's car

5. What kind of person is Jed? Use at least one example from the story in your answer. _____
    _____

6. What might Jed learn as he works at the center for seniors? Write what you think. _____
    _____

9

I don't know if he will.

Remind the student that there is not one right answer. Encourage the student to answer the question by thinking about what he or she knows about Jed and his situation. **Say,** *Based on what you know so far about Jed and his job, do you think he will start to like it?*

Explain that answering these questions will help students make sure that they understood the information they read. Answering these questions will also help them practice for other reading tests.

Have students answer the questions. Explain that, as on other tests, each multiple-choice question has one right answer, but the last two questions can be answered in different ways.

Answers to
Thinking About the Selection

1. ***C. in a room with a judge*** (Inferential—Sequence/ Setting)
2. ***A. to see the look wiped off Jed's face*** (Literal— Supporting Details/ Character)
3. ***B. He has to do community service.*** (Literal—Main Idea/Plot)
4. ***B. work at the center for seniors*** (Inferential— Making Predictions/Plot)
5. Accept all reasonable responses, including: *He must not be very happy because he acts rude to the judge. Also, Jed must not care a lot about other people because he stole a car.* (Inferential—Main Idea/ Character)
6. Accept all reasonable responses, including: *Jed might learn to have more respect for people.* (Inferential—Making Predictions/Plot)

READING LINKS

Students who enjoyed "Make Me!" might want to read the entire book, *No Pay? No Way!* Students also might enjoy reading other books about young people who change as a result of an experience or mistake.

Reading Aloud

- *As Ever, Gordy* by Mary Downing Hahn (William Morrow, 2000). [F]
- *The Ashwater Experiment* by Amy Goldman Koss (Penguin Putnam, 2001). [F]
- *Baseball Turnaround* by Matt Christopher (Little, Brown, 1997). [F]
- *Crash* by Jerry Spinelli (Knopf, 1997). [F]
- *Huckleberry Finn* by Mark Twain (Steck-Vaughn, 1991). [F]

Independent Reading

- *Don't Look Back* by Himilce Novas (Steck-Vaughn, 1997). [F]

FAMILY INVOLVEMENT

Have each student talk to an adult family member about a time when the student changed as a result of a positive experience. The student and adult should also talk about what the student learned from the situation. Volunteers can then share these stories with classmates.

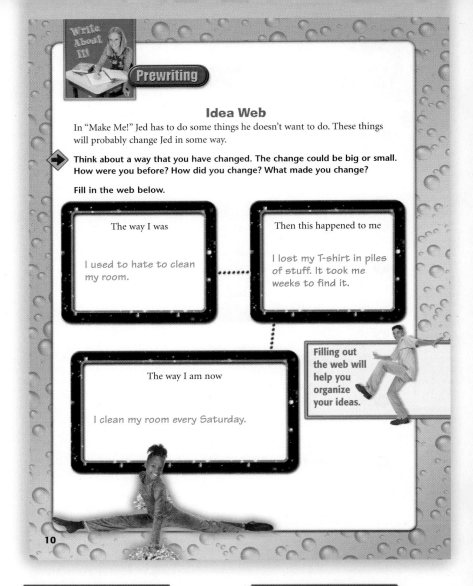

Prewriting

Idea Web

In "Make Me!" Jed has to do some things he doesn't want to do. These things will probably change Jed in some way.

➡ **Think about a way that you have changed. The change could be big or small. How were you before? How did you change? What made you change?**

Fill in the web below.

The way I was

I used to hate to clean my room.

Then this happened to me

I lost my T-shirt in piles of stuff. It took me weeks to find it.

The way I am now

I clean my room every Saturday.

Filling out the web will help you organize your ideas.

10

Before Writing

Have students brainstorm experiences that caused them to change. Write these ideas on the board. If students are having trouble generating ideas, talk about important times in their lives. Ask students to describe what they were like before those experiences and what they are like now.

Or, have students work in small groups to brainstorm ideas before they begin working independently on their webs.

During Writing

Have students refer to their idea webs. Personalize the experience for students having difficulty. **Ask,** *What do you think you might have learned? What might someone else learn by going through this experience?*

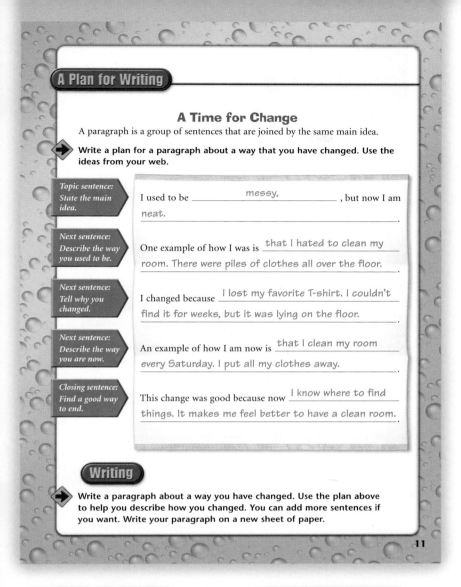

A Plan for Writing

A Time for Change

A paragraph is a group of sentences that are joined by the same main idea.

Write a plan for a paragraph about a way that you have changed. Use the ideas from your web.

Topic sentence: State the main idea.

I used to be _____ messy, _____ , but now I am neat.

Next sentence: Describe the way you used to be.

One example of how I was is _that I hated to clean my room. There were piles of clothes all over the floor._

Next sentence: Tell why you changed.

I changed because _I lost my favorite T-shirt. I couldn't find it for weeks, but it was lying on the floor._

Next sentence: Describe the way you are now.

An example of how I am now is _that I clean my room every Saturday. I put all my clothes away._

Closing sentence: Find a good way to end.

This change was good because now _I know where to find things. It makes me feel better to have a clean room._

Writing

Write a paragraph about a way you have changed. Use the plan above to help you describe how you changed. You can add more sentences if you want. Write your paragraph on a new sheet of paper.

11

After Writing

As a group, discuss students' reactions to what they have written. Encourage students to discuss why these changes have been good for them.

GROUP SHARING

When students have finished writing, organize them into groups to compare their paragraphs. Have them develop a list of the kinds of lessons that the group has learned and explain why each lesson is important.

Assessment

Portfolio Assessment
Students may want to save their informational paragraphs in their classroom portfolios.

Student Self-Assessment
Encourage students to think about their writing experience by responding to this question: *How did writing about what you learned help you to think about the good and bad experiences in your life? Why are both important?*

SCORING RUBRIC: INFORMATIONAL PARAGRAPH

SCORE 3
Topic is clearly defined, and supporting ideas are well developed. Contains clear, vivid sensory details. Writing is organized and coherent. Contains few errors in sentence structure, usage, mechanics, or spelling.

SCORE 2
Topic is defined, and supporting ideas are developed. Contains sensory details, but some are not vivid; some may not be clear. Has some degree of organization and coherence. Contains some errors in sentence structure, usage, mechanics, or spelling.

SCORE 1
Topic is not clearly defined, or paragraph is not informative. Supporting ideas are not well developed. Writing contains few or no sensory details, and most are not vivid or clear. Has minimal organization and coherence. Contains many errors in sentence structure, usage, mechanics, or spelling.

Short a

Call attention to the rule about **short a.** Read it aloud while students follow along. Use *ad* to point out that some words begin with a vowel. Use *dad* and *map* to point out that the **short a** can come in the middle of a word.

Have a volunteer read the directions aloud. Discuss the first sentence. If anyone does not understand the activity, ask a student to read the sentence, exaggerating the **short a** sound. Have students complete the second sentence independently.

Long a

Call attention to the rule about **long a.** Read it aloud while students follow along. Use *ape* to point out that some words begin with the **long a** sound. Use *tray* to point out that the **long a** can be spelled with the letters *ay.*

Have a volunteer read the directions aloud. Discuss the third sentence. If anyone does not understand the activity, ask a student to read the sentence, exaggerating the **long a** sound. Have students complete the fourth sentence independently.

Have students complete sentences five through eight independently.

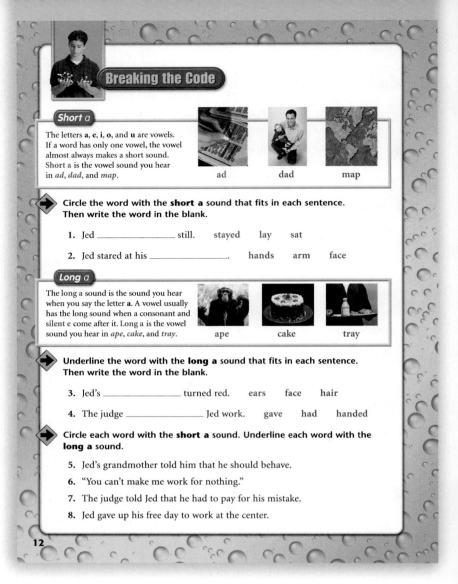

Breaking the Code

Short a

The letters **a, e, i, o,** and **u** are vowels. If a word has only one vowel, the vowel almost always makes a short sound. Short a is the vowel sound you hear in *ad, dad,* and *map.*

ad   dad   map

Circle the word with the **short a** sound that fits in each sentence. Then write the word in the blank.

1. Jed _____ still.   stayed   lay   sat

2. Jed stared at his _____.   hands   arm   face

Long a

The long a sound is the sound you hear when you say the letter **a.** A vowel usually has the long sound when a consonant and silent e come after it. Long a is the vowel sound you hear in *ape, cake,* and *tray.*

ape   cake   tray

Underline the word with the **long a** sound that fits in each sentence. Then write the word in the blank.

3. Jed's _____ turned red.   ears   face   hair

4. The judge _____ Jed work.   gave   had   handed

Circle each word with the **short a** sound. Underline each word with the **long a** sound.

5. Jed's grandmother told him that he should behave.

6. "You can't make me work for nothing."

7. The judge told Jed that he had to pay for his mistake.

8. Jed gave up his free day to work at the center.

12

Answers to Breaking the Code

1. (sat)

2. (hands)

3. face

4. gave

5. (grandmother) (that) behave

6. (can't) make

7. (that) (had) pay mistake

8. gave day (at)

RETEACHING

Identify a word with the **long a** sound. As a group, have students generate a list of related words with the **long a** sound. For example, in response to the word *jail,* students might say *cage* or *hate.* Write the words on the board.

Ask students to explain the relationship between each new word and the original word.

Repeat the activity using the **short a** sound.

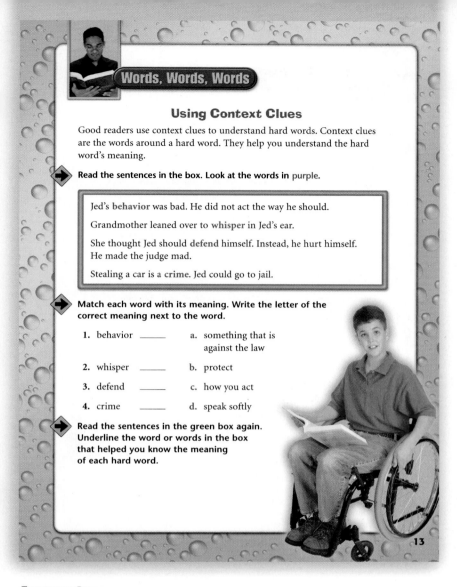

Words, Words, Words

Using Context Clues

Good readers use context clues to understand hard words. Context clues are the words around a hard word. They help you understand the hard word's meaning.

➤ Read the sentences in the box. Look at the words in purple.

> Jed's **behavior** was bad. He did not act the way he should.
>
> Grandmother leaned over to **whisper** in Jed's ear.
>
> She thought Jed should **defend** himself. Instead, he hurt himself. He made the judge mad.
>
> Stealing a car is a **crime**. Jed could go to jail.

➤ Match each word with its meaning. Write the letter of the correct meaning next to the word.

1. behavior _____   a. something that is against the law

2. whisper _____   b. protect

3. defend _____   c. how you act

4. crime _____   d. speak softly

➤ Read the sentences in the green box again. Underline the word or words in the box that helped you know the meaning of each hard word.

13

Words, Words, Words

Explain that you can often figure out the meaning of a word by how it is used in a sentence. Write the following on the board:

Jed was very upset. He clenched his fists until his fingers hurt.

Read, or ask a volunteer to read, the sentence aloud. Ask what *clenched* means. **Ask,** *What clues are in the sentences?* Elicit from students that *clenched* means "closed tightly" and that the gesture is something that someone who is upset might do. Demonstrate a clenched fist for students. Have students complete the Using Context Clues activity. Ask which words students used to understand the meaning of *behavior, whisper, defend,* and *crime.*

RETEACHING

Group students in pairs. Have each student in the pair write ten sentences. Then, have each student rewrite the sentences with one word missing. Have pairs exchange these sentences. Each student should then guess what word is missing from each sentence.

Discuss as a group why it is that some words are harder to guess than others. This is because not all sentences have enough context clues. Discuss other strategies for uncovering word meanings, such as using the dictionary or knowing word parts.

Answers to Words, Words, Words

1. **behavior** c
2. **whisper** d
3. **defend** b
4. **crime** a

Note that underlined answers will vary. Possible answers are provided. Accept any answer that demonstrates knowledge of the meaning of the word.

Jed's **behavior** was bad. He did not <u>act</u> the way he should.

Grandmother leaned over to **whisper** in Jed's ear.

She thought Jed should **defend** himself. <u>Instead, he hurt himself.</u> He made the judge mad.

Stealing a car is a **crime.** <u>Jed could go to jail.</u>

REINFORCING THE THEME

To reinforce the theme, *Onward and Upward,* discuss the word *inventions.* Have students think about how inventions change our lives. Draw a three-column chart on the board. Title the columns "Inventions," "The Way Life Used to Be," and "The Way Life Is Now." Have students generate ideas to complete the chart. Discuss how each invention has changed people's lives.

STRATEGY FOCUS

Making predictions about what will come next

Strategy

MAKING PREDICTIONS

Good readers think about what might come next in a text they are reading. When the text is nonfiction, these predictions are often based on what the reader wants to know about the topic.

Encourage students to make predictions in nonfiction texts. To make reasonable predictions, readers must think about:

- the text and what they already know about the topic, and
- what they want to know about the topic.

The activities in this unit will help students apply the strategy of making predictions. Explain that students will use this strategy as they read the selection.

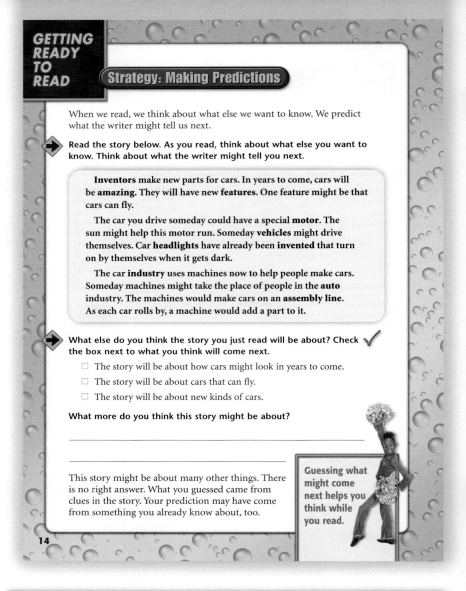

GETTING READY TO READ

Strategy: Making Predictions

When we read, we think about what else we want to know. We predict what the writer might tell us next.

➡ **Read the story below. As you read, think about what else you want to know. Think about what the writer might tell you next.**

> **Inventors** make new parts for cars. In years to come, cars will be **amazing**. They will have new **features**. One feature might be that cars can fly.
>
> The car you drive someday could have a special **motor**. The sun might help this motor run. Someday **vehicles** might drive themselves. Car **headlights** have already been **invented** that turn on by themselves when it gets dark.
>
> The car **industry** uses machines now to help people make cars. Someday machines might take the place of people in the **auto** industry. The machines would make cars on an **assembly line**. As each car rolls by, a machine would add a part to it.

➡ **What else do you think the story you just read will be about? Check ✓ the box next to what you think will come next.**

☐ The story will be about how cars might look in years to come.

☐ The story will be about cars that can fly.

☐ The story will be about new kinds of cars.

What more do you think this story might be about?

_____

_____

This story might be about many other things. There is no right answer. What you guessed came from clues in the story. Your prediction may have come from something you already know about, too.

Guessing what might come next helps you think while you read.

14

INTRODUCING THE STRATEGY

Have students read the selection. Then have them complete the questions independently or as a group. Ask students how they decided what might come next. Ask questions such as:

- What gave you clues about what else the writer might write?
- What did you know about the history of cars before you read the selection?

- What else did you want to know about the history of cars as you read the selection?
- What did you learn about the history of cars by reading the selection?

Students will make different predictions about what else the selection will be about. There is no right answer. Students will use information from the selection and from their background experience to answer the questions.

Note: The boldface words on this page are vocabulary words.

The words in the box come from the story you just read. You will see these words again in the story you are about to read.

➡ **Read the clues below. Then choose words from the box to fill in the crossword puzzle. This will help you think about each word and its meaning. The first word has been done for you.**

invented
vehicles
amazing
inventors
motor
industry
assembly
line
~~headlights~~
auto
features

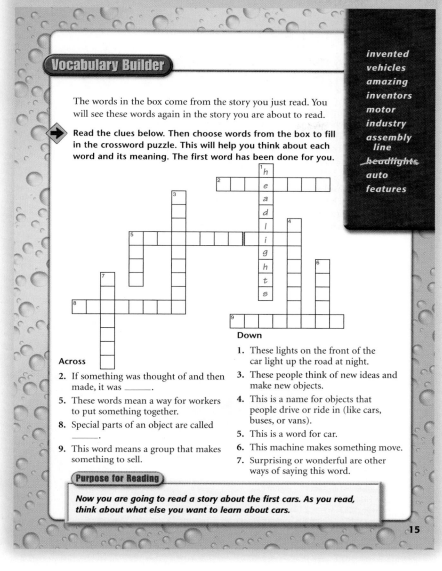

Across

2. If something was thought of and then made, it was _____.

5. These words mean a way for workers to put something together.

8. Special parts of an object are called _____.

9. This word means a group that makes something to sell.

Down

1. These lights on the front of the car light up the road at night.

3. These people think of new ideas and make new objects.

4. This is a name for objects that people drive or ride in (like cars, buses, or vans).

5. This is a word for car.

6. This machine makes something move.

7. Surprising or wonderful are other ways of saying this word.

Purpose for Reading

Now you are going to read a story about the first cars. As you read, think about what else you want to learn about cars.

15

Vocabulary Builder

Students are introduced to words that are important to their comprehension of the reading selection. The activity prepares students to understand these words as they read. Also, these vocabulary words are defined in footnotes throughout the selection.

Assessment

Check students' comprehension of the vocabulary words by having them use their own words to write a definition for each one. Have students include the words in their notebook dictionaries.

- **amazing**
- **assembly line**
- **auto**
- **features**
- **headlights**
- **industry**
- **invented**
- **inventors**
- **motor**
- **vehicles**

ADDITIONAL VOCABULARY EXTENSION

Have students guess what the selection might be about from reading the list of vocabulary words. They may enjoy drawing pictures of what they think the selection will be about.

Answers to Vocabulary Builder

Across

2. **invented**

5. **assembly line**

8. **features**

9. **industry**

Down

1. **headlights**

3. **inventors**

4. **vehicles**

5. **auto**

6. **motor**

7. **amazing**

VOCABULARY EXTENSION

Pair students. Ask the pairs to write a story in which they use the vocabulary words. Have one student start the story and include a vocabulary word. Then have the partner continue the story, using a vocabulary word. Have students continue until they have at least five vocabulary words in their story.

THE FIRST CARS

SELECTION AT A GLANCE

This selection tells about the history of cars and how they improved over time.

INTERESTING FACTS

In most states, students can look forward to driving a car when they are 16 years old. They might be interested to know that if they lived in Europe, they would probably have to wait a couple more years to get behind the wheel. The minimum driving age in Western European countries is 17 or 18.

Before Reading

INTRODUCING THE SELECTION

Tell students that the Model T was built in 1908. Explain that while the Model T looked a bit like today's cars, it didn't have extra features that today's cars have. Draw a two-column chart on the board. Write "Model T" at the top of the first column. At the top of the second column, write "Today's Cars." Have students brainstorm a list of features that the Model T must have had. Write students' ideas in the first column. Then have students generate a list of features that have been added to cars over time. Write those in the second column. Have students explain why they think those features were added to cars.

16

THE FIRST CARS

THE FIRST CARS

Cars play an important part in our lives. When cars were **invented**, they were just a new way to get places. Today, cars are used for much more. There are **vehicles** for special jobs. We feel safer when we see a police car on the street. Cabs and vans take us places. Some people drive race cars for fun. Many people choose a car because they think it looks cool.

It's hard to think of life without cars, yet we have had cars for only about a hundred years. As you read, you will learn about the history of American cars. Who made them? How were they built? Why did they change? Read on to find out about these **amazing** machines.

> 1. What will you read about in this story? Write what you think.

invented (ihn VEHN tehd) *adjective* Something that has been invented has been thought about and then made for the first time.
vehicles (VEE uh kuhlz) *noun* Vehicles are things that people drive or ride in.
amazing (uh MAYZ ihng) *adjective* Something that is surprising or wonderful is amazing.

16

During Reading

PURPOSE FOR READING

Students read to make predictions about what they will learn next about the first cars.

APPLYING THE STRATEGY

Have students read the selection in the *Workout Book*. Explain that they are to answer the questions in the boxes as they read the selection. Remind them that answering these questions will help them think about what they are going to read next.

Possible Responses

Question 1

It will probably be about what different kinds of cars do.

This student is relying on what he read in the first paragraph to answer the question. Ask him to use the title as well.

The first cars.

This student is relying on the title to answer the question. She may be afraid of being wrong. **Say,** *When we make predictions, it's okay if some are not correct.*

The Car Is Born

Who made the first car? It's hard to know. Many **inventors** tried during the 1880s and 1890s. Some people say that Karl Benz was the first. He was a German inventor. He built a car in 1886. This car did not look like today's cars. It had three wheels. It was made from a bike and a **motor**.

In the United States, the Duryea brothers had read about Karl Benz. In 1893, they made a car from a wagon. They built a motor and put it on the wagon. They called it the Motor Wagon. Three years later, the Duryea brothers made thirteen Motor Wagons. That was the beginning of the car **industry**.

Henry Ford and the Model T

An American, Henry Ford, was important to the car industry. He did not invent the first car, but he did think of better ways to make cars.

Ford built the first Model T car in 1908. This car looked more like today's cars. It had four wheels and a roof. People liked the Model T so much that they gave it a special name. They called it the Tin Lizzie.

> 2. Why do you think people kept trying to build better cars?

Before the Model T, cars were built one at a time. It cost a lot of money to make each one. Only a few people had the money to buy these cars.

---

inventors (ihn VEHN tuhrz) *noun* Inventors are people who think of new ideas and make new things.
motor (MOHT uhr) *noun* A motor is a machine that makes something move.
industry (IHN duhs tree) *noun* An industry is a group that makes something to sell.

17

Question 2

For safety.

Ask this student for clarification. **Say,** *I know what you mean, but could you say more about what you're thinking?*

My mom and dad wouldn't buy a new car unless it was better than their last car.

This student indirectly answers the question by making a personal connection. Encourage the student to elaborate on what she is thinking. **Say,** *Tell how your example with your mom and dad helps explain why you think people kept trying to build better cars.*

Divide the class into five groups. Have each group read a different section of "The First Cars." When students have finished reading, have each group explain to the other groups what they learned in their section. Begin with the group that read the first section in the selection. When each group has finished its discussion, **say,** *What is another header that the author might have used for this section?*

A Better Way

In 1913, Ford thought of a better way to build cars. His workers would build them on a moving **assembly line**. In an assembly line, each worker adds one part. Workers could build each Model T quickly. It did not cost as much money to build each car. So, Ford could sell Model Ts for a low price. Many Americans bought them.

The Model T sold very well. In 19 years, Ford made more than 15 million cars. Over the years, he made the Model T better. He gave it a new motor and **headlights**.

3. What do you think happened when cars cost less?

assembly line (uh SEHM blee LYN) *noun* An assembly line is a moving belt like the ones you see at the store. The belt is used to move things. Each worker adds a different part to the thing.
headlights (HEHD lyts) *noun* Headlights are the front lights of a car that light up the road at night.

18

Possible Responses

Question 3

More people could afford to buy them.

This student shows a good understanding of what happened when cars were produced in greater numbers and sold at lower prices.

Cars could be built more quickly.

This response indicates that the student understood a detail in the selection, but may have missed the main idea. **Say,** *Yes, cars were built more quickly. As a result, cars were cheaper. What happened when cars were cheaper?*

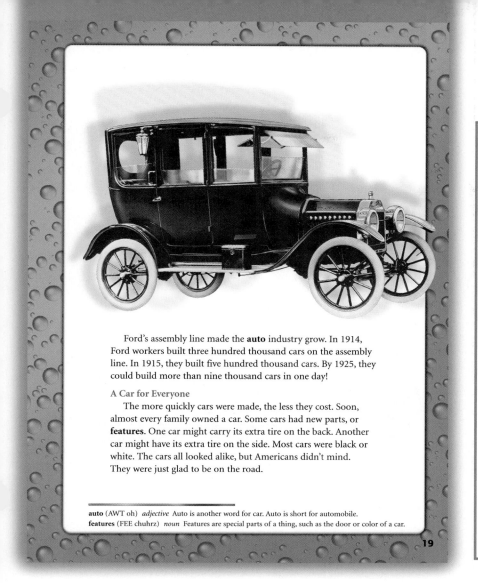

Ford's assembly line made the **auto** industry grow. In 1914, Ford workers built three hundred thousand cars on the assembly line. In 1915, they built five hundred thousand cars. By 1925, they could build more than nine thousand cars in one day!

A Car for Everyone

The more quickly cars were made, the less they cost. Soon, almost every family owned a car. Some cars had new parts, or **features**. One car might carry its extra tire on the back. Another car might have its extra tire on the side. Most cars were black or white. The cars all looked alike, but Americans didn't mind. They were just glad to be on the road.

---

auto (AWT oh) *adjective* Auto is another word for car. Auto is short for automobile.
features (FEE chuhrz) *noun* Features are special parts of a thing, such as the door or color of a car.

19

Notes

If you have Spanish-speaking students in class, have them help you explain a bit of car trivia to the rest of the class. Tell students that when a company called General Motors tried to sell its new car in Puerto Rico, it ran into some unexpected trouble. The name of the car, the Nova, translates into something in Spanish that kept many Puerto Ricans from wanting to buy the car. Ask your Spanish-speaking students to tell the class what "No va" means in Spanish. (It means "does not go.") Ask students who speak other languages what such a car would be called in their language.

RECIPROCAL TEACHING

Question

Have pairs of students work together to generate a list of five questions that can be answered by the selection. Once questions are written, have each pair join with a second pair of students. Have each pair in a group alternate asking the other pair one of their questions. Encourage students to try to answer the questions without looking in the selection. However, if students are unsure of the answer, have them search for the answer in the selection.

After Reading

It is very important to have students read and discuss the predictions they have written in the boxes.

DISCUSSING THE RESPONSES

- Give as many students as possible a chance to tell what they wrote in one of the boxes.
- Have students explain what they were thinking when they wrote.
- Ask students how making predictions helped them think about the selection.

RETEACHING

Have students who have not written in the boxes or who are having difficulty with the activity create a timeline of the events in the selection. On their timelines, have students list the years that are discussed in the selection. Then, under the appropriate year, have them briefly write down why that year is important in the history of cars. Students can do this independently or in small groups. You might also have the entire class make a big timeline to display on the classroom wall.

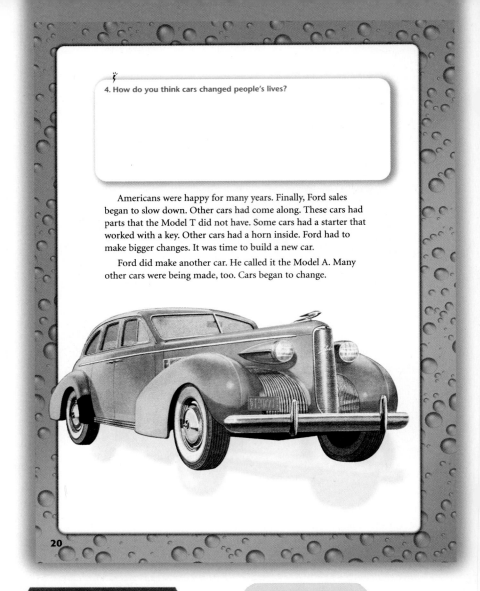

4. How do you think cars changed people's lives?

Americans were happy for many years. Finally, Ford sales began to slow down. Other cars had come along. These cars had parts that the Model T did not have. Some cars had a starter that worked with a key. Other cars had a horn inside. Ford had to make bigger changes. It was time to build a new car.

Ford did make another car. He called it the Model A. Many other cars were being made, too. Cars began to change.

20

Assessment

Informal Assessment
To assess students' comprehension of the selection, use their responses in the boxes and their discussion of their responses.

Student Self-Assessment
Encourage students to think about their reading experience by responding to this question: *How did answering the questions in the boxes help you think about what you would be reading next?*

Possible Responses

Question 4

Things got better.

This student has not provided any detail. Encourage the student to elaborate. Ask, *In what ways did things get better?*

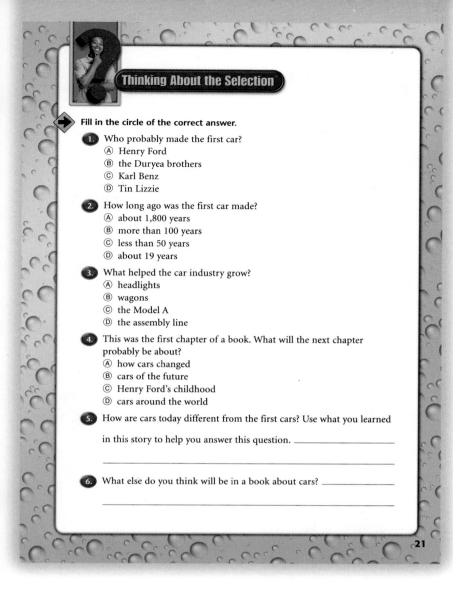

→ Fill in the circle of the correct answer.

1. Who probably made the first car?
   - Ⓐ Henry Ford
   - Ⓑ the Duryea brothers
   - Ⓒ Karl Benz
   - Ⓓ Tin Lizzie

2. How long ago was the first car made?
   - Ⓐ about 1,800 years
   - Ⓑ more than 100 years
   - Ⓒ less than 50 years
   - Ⓓ about 19 years

3. What helped the car industry grow?
   - Ⓐ headlights
   - Ⓑ wagons
   - Ⓒ the Model A
   - Ⓓ the assembly line

4. This was the first chapter of a book. What will the next chapter probably be about?
   - Ⓐ how cars changed
   - Ⓑ cars of the future
   - Ⓒ Henry Ford's childhood
   - Ⓓ cars around the world

5. How are cars today different from the first cars? Use what you learned in this story to help you answer this question. _____
   _____

6. What else do you think will be in a book about cars? _____
   _____

21

It probably wasn't as much fun because no one rode their horses anymore. I would rather ride on a horse than in a car.

This student offers a personal reaction, and draws a logical conclusion based on that reaction. Ask, *Do you think everyone missed riding horses to get from place to place?*

Explain that answering these questions will help students check their comprehension. Answering these questions will also help them practice for other reading tests.

Have students answer the questions. Explain that, as on other tests, each multiple-choice question has one right answer, but the last two questions can be answered in different ways.

Answers to Thinking About the Selection

1. **C. Karl Benz** (Literal—Sequence/Detail)
2. **B. more than 100 years** (Literal—Main Idea)
3. **D. the assembly line** (Literal—Cause/Effect)
4. **A. how cars changed** (Inferential—Making Predictions)
5. Accept all reasonable responses, including: *Today cars have four wheels. Cars come in many different colors. Most people have a car.* (Inferential—Main Idea)
6. Accept all reasonable responses, including: *A book about cars will probably talk about different kinds of cars today. It will probably talk about how cars work.* (Inferential—Making Predictions)

Students who enjoyed "The First Cars" might also enjoy reading the entire book, *Follow That Car!*. Students might also enjoy reading other books about cars or inventions.

Reading Aloud

- *Almost Famous* by David Getz (Holt, 1994). [F]
- *Cars and How They Work* by George Cruickshank (DK Publishing, 1992). [NF]
- *Girls Think of Everything* by Catherine Thimmesh (Houghton Mifflin, 2000). [NF]
- *Technology* by Roger Bridgman (DK Publishing, 1999). [NF]
- *The Time Machine* by H.G. Wells (Steck-Vaughn, 1991). [F]

FAMILY INVOLVEMENT

Have each student talk to an adult family member about something that was invented during the adult's lifetime. Tell the students to ask about how life was different before the invention came along. Compile a list of the inventions. Ask students to think about what inventions they couldn't live without—even though some adults they know had to.

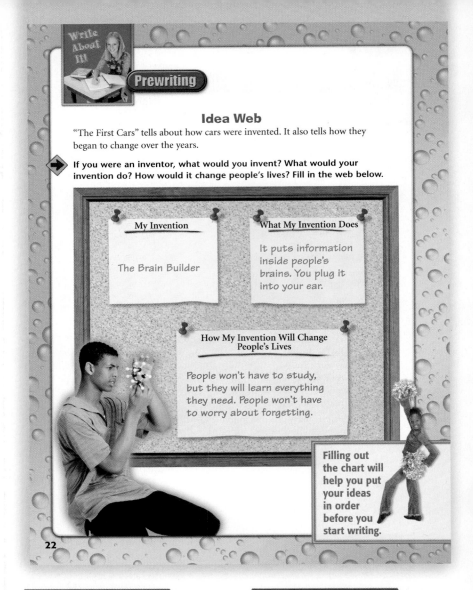

Prewriting

Idea Web

"The First Cars" tells about how cars were invented. It also tells how they began to change over the years.

If you were an inventor, what would you invent? What would your invention do? How would it change people's lives? Fill in the web below.

My Invention

The Brain Builder

What My Invention Does

It puts information inside people's brains. You plug it into your ear.

How My Invention Will Change People's Lives

People won't have to study, but they will learn everything they need. People won't have to worry about forgetting.

Filling out the chart will help you put your ideas in order before you start writing.

22

Before Writing

Have students brainstorm machines that have not been invented, but that they would like to have. Write these ideas on the board. If students are having trouble generating ideas, talk about how they would like to change their lives. How could a machine make those changes happen? How would that machine work?

Or, have students work in small groups to brainstorm ideas before they begin working independently on their charts.

During Writing

Have students refer to their idea charts. Personalize the experience for students having difficulty. **Ask,** *If a machine could do anything you wanted, what would it do?* or *How could a new invention change the way people live?*

After Writing

Discuss students' reactions to what they have written. Have them help each other with new ways to make their stories more interesting—and make their inventions better.

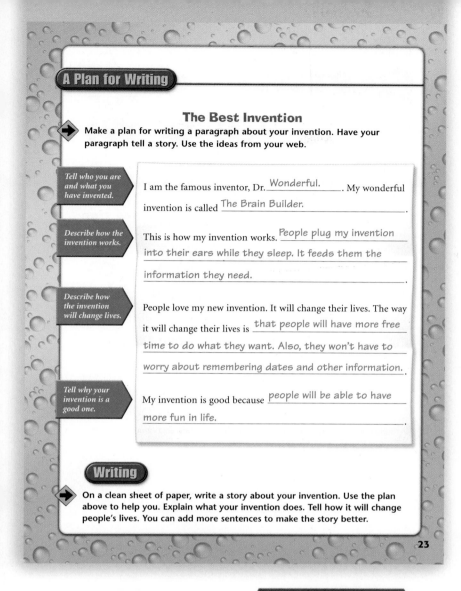

A Plan for Writing

The Best Invention

Make a plan for writing a paragraph about your invention. Have your paragraph tell a story. Use the ideas from your web.

Tell who you are and what you have invented.

I am the famous inventor, Dr. _Wonderful._ . My wonderful invention is called _The Brain Builder._

Describe how the invention works.

This is how my invention works. _People plug my invention into their ears while they sleep. It feeds them the information they need._

Describe how the invention will change lives.

People love my new invention. It will change their lives. The way it will change their lives is _that people will have more free time to do what they want. Also, they won't have to worry about remembering dates and other information._

Tell why your invention is a good one.

My invention is good because _people will be able to have more fun in life._

Writing

On a clean sheet of paper, write a story about your invention. Use the plan above to help you. Explain what your invention does. Tell how it will change people's lives. You can add more sentences to make the story better.

23

GROUP SHARING

When students have finished the writing activity, group them in pairs. Have students read their stories to each other. You might also generate a list of the kinds of inventions that the group thought of. Have them also list how each invention would change people's lives.

Assessment

Portfolio Assessment
Students may want to save their narrative paragraphs in their classroom portfolios.

Student Self-Assessment
Encourage students to think about their writing experience by responding to this question: *How did writing your story help you to think of new inventions that you might really want to build some day? Why do machines affect people's lives so much?*

Breaking the Code

Short e

Read aloud the section on **short e** while students read along. Use *eggs* to point out that some **short e** words begin with a vowel. Use *head* and *bell* to point out that the **short e** can come in the middle of a word. As you read the words, exaggerate the **short e** sound.

Have a volunteer read the directions aloud. Discuss the first sentence with the group. Have students complete the second sentence independently.

Long e

Call attention to the rule about the **long e** sound. Read it aloud while students follow along. Use *eat* to point out that some words begin with the **long e** sound. Use *feet* and *key* to point out that the **long e** is often spelled with two vowels. As you read the words, exaggerate the **long e** sound.

Call on a volunteer to read the directions aloud. Discuss the third sentence with the group. Have students complete the fourth sentence independently.

Have students complete sentences five through eight independently.

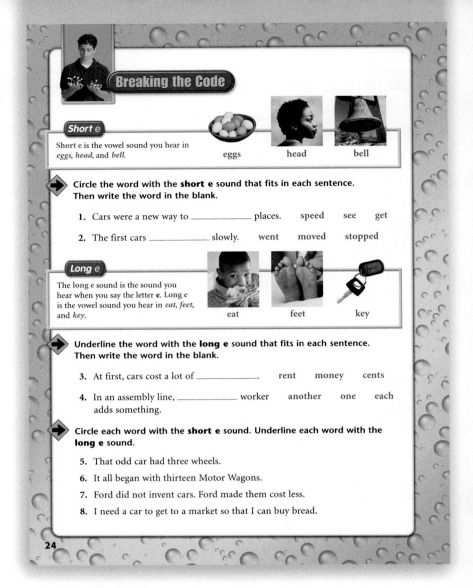

Breaking the Code

Short e

Short e is the vowel sound you hear in *eggs*, *head*, and *bell*.

eggs   head   bell

Circle the word with the **short e** sound that fits in each sentence. Then write the word in the blank.

1. Cars were a new way to _____ places.   speed   see   get

2. The first cars _____ slowly.   went   moved   stopped

Long e

The long e sound is the sound you hear when you say the letter **e**. Long e is the vowel sound you hear in *eat*, *feet*, and *key*.

eat   feet   key

Underline the word with the **long e** sound that fits in each sentence. Then write the word in the blank.

3. At first, cars cost a lot of _____.   rent   money   cents

4. In an assembly line, _____ worker adds something.   another   one   each

Circle each word with the **short e** sound. Underline each word with the **long e** sound.

5. That odd car had three wheels.
6. It all began with thirteen Motor Wagons.
7. Ford did not invent cars. Ford made them cost less.
8. I need a car to get to a market so that I can buy bread.

24

Answers to Breaking the Code

1. (get)
2. (went)
3. money
4. each
5. three wheels
6. began thirteen
7. (invent) (them) (less)
8. need (get) (market) (bread)

RETEACHING

Group students in pairs. Have each pair write these three words across the top of a sheet of paper: *streamlined, satellites, features.* Under each word, have students write two column headers: *short e* and *long e.* Then, ask students to write as many *short e* and *long e* words as they can think of that are made from only the letters within that word. For example, under the *long e* column for the word *streamlined,* students might write the word *neat.*

Understanding Compound Words

Some long words are made from two smaller words. These are called *compound words*. In the story you read, the word *headlights* is a compound word. It is made of two smaller words.

head + lights = headlights

These smaller words help you know the meaning of the long word. Look at the words *head* and *lights*. They show that *headlights* means "lights in the front."

➤ **Read the story in the box. Look at the words in** purple**. They are compound words.**

We spent the **afternoon outdoors**. We sat in the front yard near the **sidewalk**. We watched the sun go down. It was a pretty **sunset**. We saw **fireflies** wink their lights off and on in the **moonlight**. Soon it was **bedtime**. It was the end of a perfect day.

➤ **Fill in the chart below. Write the two smaller words that make each compound word. Then write the meaning of the compound word.**

Compound Word	Smaller Words		Meaning
afternoon			
outdoors			
sidewalk			
sunset			
fireflies			
moonlight			
bedtime			

25

Answers to Words, Words, Words

Compound Word	Smaller Words		Meaning
afternoon	after	noon	after the middle of the day
outdoors	out	doors	outside the house, out the door
sidewalk	side	walk	the walk by the side of the yard
sunset	sun	set	when the sun goes down
fireflies	fire	flies	bugs that light up
moonlight	moon	light	the light of the moon
bedtime	bed	time	time to go to bed

Words, Words, Words

Write the word *campground* on the board. Ask students what two words they see. Explain that when two words are put together, they become a compound word. Write the following words on the board:

finger   *tip*

hand   *shake*

Ask students what two words the small words make (*fingertip* and *handshake*).

Then ask students to define or demonstrate *fingertip* and *handshake*. Lead them to understand that the definition of a compound word uses some aspect of the meanings of the two smaller words. Have students complete the Understanding Compound Words activity.

RETEACHING

Write the following list of words on the board:

news   *boat*

home   *cup*

house   *hood*

made   *tea*

paper   *neighbor*

Challenge students to come up with five compound words from this list. Then, as a group, define these compound words using the students' own words.

REINFORCING THE THEME

To reinforce the theme, *Onward and Upward,* have students discuss how problems are sometimes opportunities. Have students think about problems they have had with friends, school, or activities. Then have them think about what they learned from these problems. Have students draw a line down a piece of paper, write a problem on the left side, and write how that problem was a hidden opportunity on the right side. Tell students the story they will read is about a boy who learns from a problem.

STRATEGY FOCUS

Recognizing the sequence of events

Strategy

RECOGNIZING SEQUENCE

Readers have to recognize what happens first, next, and last to understand relationships between events, such as cause and effect.

Emphasize sequence by having students:

- think about actions for which they have directions (such as recipes or games), and

- discuss why the sequence of directions is important.

The activities in this unit will help students apply the strategy of recognizing sequence.

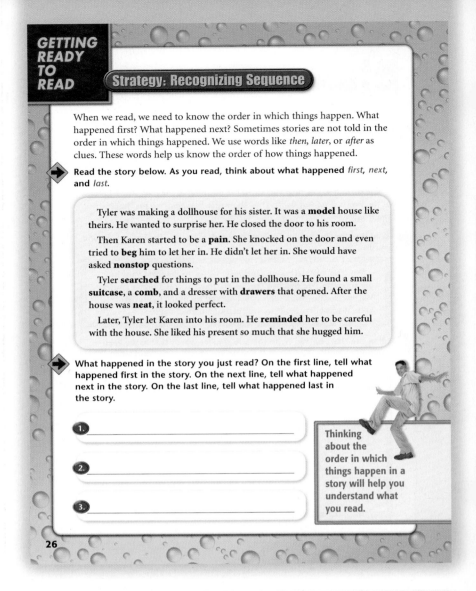

GETTING READY TO READ

Strategy: Recognizing Sequence

When we read, we need to know the order in which things happen. What happened first? What happened next? Sometimes stories are not told in the order in which things happened. We use words like *then, later,* or *after* as clues. These words help us know the order of how things happened.

➡ **Read the story below. As you read, think about what happened *first, next,* and *last.***

> Tyler was making a dollhouse for his sister. It was a **model** house like theirs. He wanted to surprise her. He closed the door to his room.
>
> Then Karen started to be a **pain**. She knocked on the door and even tried to **beg** him to let her in. He didn't let her in. She would have asked **nonstop** questions.
>
> Tyler **searched** for things to put in the dollhouse. He found a small **suitcase**, a **comb**, and a dresser with **drawers** that opened. After the house was **neat**, it looked perfect.
>
> Later, Tyler let Karen into his room. He **reminded** her to be careful with the house. She liked his present so much that she hugged him.

➡ **What happened in the story you just read? On the first line, tell what happened first in the story. On the next line, tell what happened next in the story. On the last line, tell what happened last in the story.**

1. _____

2. _____

3. _____

Thinking about the order in which things happen in a story will help you understand what you read.

26

INTRODUCING THE STRATEGY

Have students read the story. Then have them fill in the three boxes independently or as a group. Ask students what information or words from the story helped them decide what happened first, next, and last. Ask questions such as:

- How can words like *then* and *later* help you decide the order of events?

- Are stories always told in sequence? Can you give an example to support your answer?

Explain that different students might write different words in the boxes. Using the exact words is not as important as understanding the events that happened first, next, and last.

Tell students they will use this strategy as they read the story.

Note: The boldface words on this page are vocabulary words.

The words in the box come from the story you just read. You will see these words again in the story you are about to read.

Complete each sentence with one of the words from the box.

beg
comb
drawers
model
neat
nonstop
pain
reminded
searched
suitcase

1. I am the word _____pain_____. I am a person who makes you angry.

2. I am the word _____. You can take me on a trip. I am made of two smaller words.

3. I am the word _____. I'm what the dog might do to get food at dinner.

4. I am the word _____. I have teeth but do not bite. I can make your hair look good.

5. I am the word _____. I am another way of saying that something is in order. I rhyme with sweet.

6. We are the word _____. You can keep clothes in us.

7. I am the word _____. I go all the time and never stop.

8. I am the word _____. I am something small that looks like something big.

9. I am the word _____. I am what you did when you looked and looked for something. I start with the letter s.

10. I am the word _____. I am what you did when you told someone something to help them remember it.

Purpose for Reading

Now you are going to read a story about two stepbrothers, James and Tyrone. James is upset. As you read, think about what happened to make James feel this way.

27

Answers to Vocabulary Builder

1. **The first answer is provided for students. pain**

2. **suitcase**

3. **beg**

4. **comb**

5. **neat**

6. **drawers**

7. **nonstop**

8. **model**

9. **searched**

10. **reminded**

VOCABULARY EXTENSION

Play a game of word charades in small groups or as a whole class activity. Have each student select a word and act it out or draw a picture of it. Have the other students guess the word.

Students are introduced to vocabulary words from the story they will read. Reading the words in context and completing the activity will help students understand the words when they encounter them in the reading selection. For additional reinforcement, the vocabulary words are defined in footnotes throughout the story.

Assessment

Check students' comprehension by having them make flashcards of the words and their definitions. Challenge students to guess the word by looking only at its definition.

- **beg**
- **comb**
- **drawers**
- **model**
- **neat**
- **nonstop**
- **pain**
- **reminded**
- **searched**
- **suitcase**

Missing!

SELECTION AT A GLANCE

In this story, a boy named James is worried when he thinks his new stepbrother might have run away.

INTERESTING FACTS

A stepfamily is a family in which one or both of the adults bring children from a previous relationship. It is difficult to determine how many stepfamilies there are in the United States because the Census Bureau, Americans' source for most information about our population, does not estimate this. Other researchers, though, estimate that one out of three Americans is now a member of a stepfamily.

Before Reading

INTRODUCING THE SELECTION

Draw a timeline on the board. Above the middle write, "James wakes up in a quiet house." Above the left end of the timeline write, "What happened before?" Above the right end write, "What happened after?" Tell students that in the story they will read, James wakes up to an unusually quiet house. What might have happened first to make the house so quiet? What might happen after James wakes up? Have students think about a few different possible sequences of events before they begin reading.

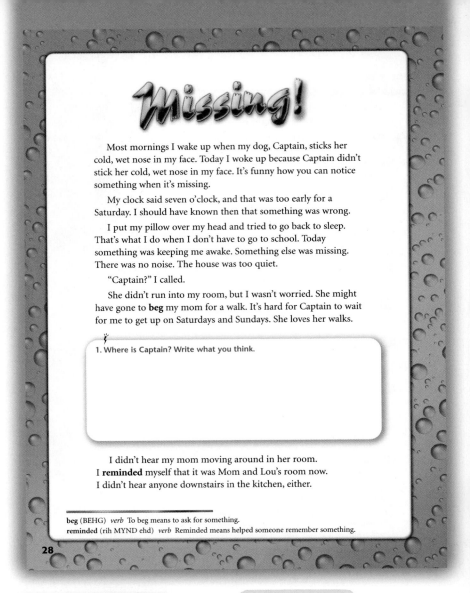

Missing!

Most mornings I wake up when my dog, Captain, sticks her cold, wet nose in my face. Today I woke up because Captain didn't stick her cold, wet nose in my face. It's funny how you can notice something when it's missing.

My clock said seven o'clock, and that was too early for a Saturday. I should have known then that something was wrong.

I put my pillow over my head and tried to go back to sleep. That's what I do when I don't have to go to school. Today something was keeping me awake. Something else was missing. There was no noise. The house was too quiet.

"Captain?" I called.

She didn't run into my room, but I wasn't worried. She might have gone to **beg** my mom for a walk. It's hard for Captain to wait for me to get up on Saturdays and Sundays. She loves her walks.

1. Where is Captain? Write what you think.

I didn't hear my mom moving around in her room. I **reminded** myself that it was Mom and Lou's room now. I didn't hear anyone downstairs in the kitchen, either.

beg (BEHG) *verb* To beg means to ask for something.
reminded (rih MYND ehd) *verb* Reminded means helped someone remember something.

28

During Reading

PURPOSE FOR READING

Students read to find out what happened to make James upset.

APPLYING THE STRATEGY

Have students read the story in the *Workout Book*. Explain that they will answer questions while they read the story. Remind them that answering these questions will help them think about the sequence of events in the story.

Possible Responses

Question 1

I think Captain probably ran away.

The student makes a reasonable inference based on the text of the story so far.

He's not home.

Encourage the student to elaborate on this response. **Say,** *What in the story makes you think so?*

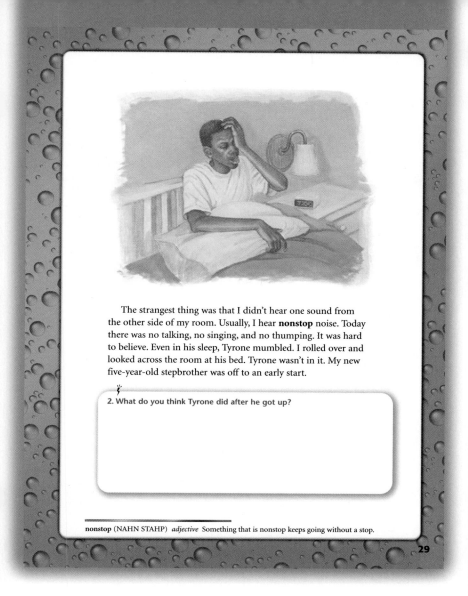

The strangest thing was that I didn't hear one sound from the other side of my room. Usually, I hear **nonstop** noise. Today there was no talking, no singing, and no thumping. It was hard to believe. Even in his sleep, Tyrone mumbled. I rolled over and looked across the room at his bed. Tyrone wasn't in it. My new five-year-old stepbrother was off to an early start.

2. What do you think Tyrone did after he got up?

---

nonstop (NAHN STAHP) *adjective* Something that is nonstop keeps going without a stop.

Strategy Tip

As students read, have them make a timeline of story events. Remind them that some of the events on the timeline might not take place during the morning of the story, but might be details about what happened to James before the story started.

FICTION READING STRATEGY

Setting

Explain that setting describes where a story takes place. In this story, the setting is important from the first paragraph when James awakes in a quiet house.

Have students draw pictures of one of the places described in the story. Have them share their pictures with the rest of the class. Discuss what students noticed about the setting.

Choose other stories that your students know and ask them to discuss the settings for those stories.

Question 2

Maybe he took the dog out for a walk.

This student connects information from the story to generate this response.

Maybe he is sick.

While there is not information to support this, the story does not contradict this conclusion either. Encourage this student to explain this response. **Say,** *What in the story makes you think so?*

If students are having difficulty answering the questions in the boxes, remind them to think about what they are reading. **Say,** *The questions are there to help you think about what you are reading. If you can't think of an answer, re-read the paragraphs before the question, then write your answer. Your answer will come from thinking about the story.*

"Good," I said to myself. I turned over to go back to sleep.

Only it was no good trying to go back to sleep. All that quiet was keeping me awake. Being awake made me hungry. Finally, I had to give up on sleeping late. I went downstairs to take care of my growling stomach. I found a note on the kitchen table. It read:

> 6:55 A.M.
>
> Dear James,
> Lou and I took Captain for a run in the park. We will grab breakfast out. Please keep an eye on Tyrone when he gets up.
>
> Love, Mom

I wondered why she wrote "when he gets up." He was already up, but where was he?

3. Did James's mom and Lou leave before or after Tyrone got up? Tell why you think so.

There was no way around it. The kid was a **pain** when he was there and a pain when he wasn't.

I thought maybe he was hiding.

"Tyrone?" I called. "Stop playing around. It's too early for games."

---

pain (PAYN) *noun* A pain is someone who makes other people angry.

Possible Responses

Question 3

I don't know.

This student has missed a few important sequence details in the story. **Say,** *It can help to re-read if you can't answer a question. Read the first two paragraphs and the note from James's mom. What clues tell you about when they left for their walk?*

Where's Tyrone?

This student does not answer the question, but shows comprehension of the story with this question. Encourage this student to elaborate further on both the question and the response. **Say,** *That is a good question. Where do you think he might be?*

Sound travels in an old house like ours, so Tyrone should have heard me. He was always making a lot of noise. I should have been able to hear him, even if he was hiding.

I stuck my head out the front door. "Tyrone?"

He wasn't in the front yard. He wasn't in the back yard, either.

My stomach growled again, louder this time. I needed to eat something.

---

4. What might happen next?

"Games are only fun if both people want to play, Tyrone," I yelled.

There was still no sound.

I **searched** every hiding place I could think of downstairs. Then, I went up to my mom's room. Tyrone wasn't anywhere. By the time I got to my room, I was starting to get a bad feeling.

---

searched (SURCHD) *verb* Searched means looked for someone or something.

31

Students for whom English is not a first language may benefit from hearing the story read aloud. Pair students for reading aloud or have students take turns reading aloud to the group. Begin by reading aloud the first section, modeling the way good readers adjust their intonation, pace, and volume to make what they read easier for their audience to understand.

RECIPROCAL TEACHING

Clarify

Encourage students to think actively about what text clues help them answer questions and understand the sequence of what they read.

Model for students how you clarify while reading. Demonstrate specific strategies, such as using context to understand unknown words or re-reading.

Question 4

He will eat.

This is a reasonable conclusion based on the text that immediately precedes the question. Encourage this student to think about the larger events in the story as well. **Say,** *What else do you think he will do next?*

He will keep looking for Tyrone because he is getting worried.

This response predicts the sequence of events in the story. The additional explanation for the character motivation demonstrates that the student is connecting with the text.

After Reading

It is very important to have students read and discuss the story and their responses to the questions in the boxes.

DISCUSSING THE RESPONSES

- As a whole group or in pairs, have students share their responses to the questions.

- Ask students to support their responses. Say, *What in the story made you answer the question that way?*

- Ask students how thinking about sequence helped them understand what they read.

RETEACHING

For those students who are having difficulty, read the story aloud as a group, having students take turns reading and sharing their responses.

As you read together, complete a sequence of events timeline for the story. Use the following model:

- First, James woke up.

- Something was different. What was different was that _____.

- James did not know where both _____ and _____ were.

- He found a note. The note told him that _____.

- Then, he was worried because he did not know _____.

Tyrone's side of the room was too **neat**. The blanket was pulled up over the bed. There weren't any crayons or books on the floor. Nothing was on his table. There was no **comb**, no flashlight, and no money jar. There weren't any of those toy people he always played with.

I knew what I'd find before I started opening **drawers**. His clothes were gone. His **suitcase** wasn't in the closet. I'm not sure why I looked under my bed. I didn't find Tyrone. Instead I found the two missing pieces of my favorite **model** ship. They were the pieces I'd thought Tyrone had taken. I sat on my bed and put my head in my hands.

This would never have happened if my mom hadn't married Tyrone's dad, Lou. Tyrone and his dad would still be living in the next state. Tyrone would be making all that noise in his own room instead of mine. He wouldn't be my new stepbrother.

He wouldn't have run away.

neat (NEET) *adjective* Neat means clean.
comb (KOHM) *noun* A comb is a tool used for brushing hair.
drawers (DRAW uhrz) *noun* Drawers are boxes in a dresser that can be pulled out. They are used to keep clothes in.
suitcase (SOOT kays) *noun* A suitcase is a box to put clothes in. It is used when traveling.
model (MAHD l) *adjective* Model means a smaller form of something.

32

Assessment

Informal Assessment
To assess students' understanding, use their written responses in the boxes and their oral explanations for what they wrote.

Student Self-Assessment
Encourage students to think about their own reading experience by responding to this question: *How did answering the questions while you read help you think about what happened to James?*

Notes

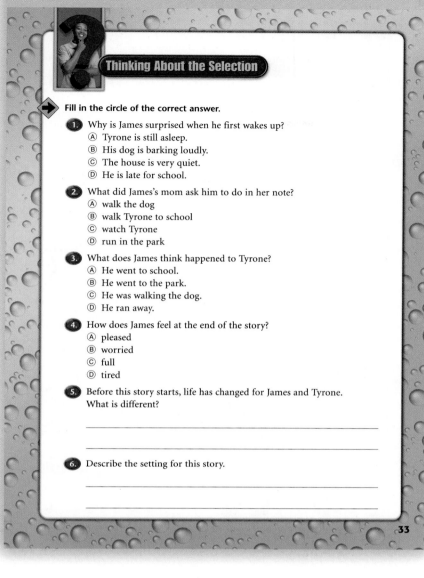

Fill in the circle of the correct answer.

1. Why is James surprised when he first wakes up?
   - Ⓐ Tyrone is still asleep.
   - Ⓑ His dog is barking loudly.
   - Ⓒ The house is very quiet.
   - Ⓓ He is late for school.

2. What did James's mom ask him to do in her note?
   - Ⓐ walk the dog
   - Ⓑ walk Tyrone to school
   - Ⓒ watch Tyrone
   - Ⓓ run in the park

3. What does James think happened to Tyrone?
   - Ⓐ He went to school.
   - Ⓑ He went to the park.
   - Ⓒ He was walking the dog.
   - Ⓓ He ran away.

4. How does James feel at the end of the story?
   - Ⓐ pleased
   - Ⓑ worried
   - Ⓒ full
   - Ⓓ tired

5. Before this story starts, life has changed for James and Tyrone. What is different?

   _____

   _____

6. Describe the setting for this story.

   _____

   _____

33

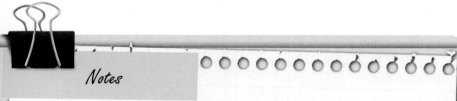

Notes

Thinking About the Selection

Explain that answering these questions will help students check their comprehension. Answering these questions will also help them practice for other reading tests.

Have students answer the questions. Explain that, as on other tests, each multiple-choice question has one right answer, but the last two questions can be answered in different ways.

Answers to Thinking About the Selection

1. ***C. The house is very quiet.*** (Literal—Cause-Effect/ Setting)
2. ***C. watch Tyrone*** (Literal— Supporting Details/Plot)
3. ***D. He ran away.*** (Inferential—Main Idea/Plot)
4. ***B. worried*** (Inferential— Sequence/Character)
5. Accept all reasonable responses, including: *James's mom married Tyrone's dad and now the boys are stepbrothers.* (Literal—Main Idea/Plot)
6. Accept all reasonable responses, including: *The story takes place in an old house where James shares a room with his new stepbrother.* (Literal—Main Idea/Setting)

Students who enjoyed "Missing!" might want to read the entire book, *Missing Pieces.* Students might enjoy reading other books about young people in conflict with family members.

Reading Aloud

- *Matilda* by Roald Dahl (Penguin, 1998). [F]
- *The Pinballs* by Betsy Byars (HarperCollins, 1987). [F]
- *Shades of Gray* by Carolyn Reeder (Simon & Schuster, 1999). [F]
- *Step by Wicked Step* by Anne Fine (Bantam Doubleday Dell, 1997). [F]
- *Superfudge* by Judy Blume (Bantam Doubleday Dell, 1981). [F]
- *Cinderella/That Awful Cinderella* by Alvin Granowsky (Steck-Vaughn, 1994). [F]

Independent Reading

- *Amber Brown Wants Extra Credit* by Paula Danzinger (Scholastic, 1997). [F]
- *Andy and Tamika* by David Adler (Harcourt, 1999). [F]

FAMILY INVOLVEMENT

Have each student talk with an adult family member about a conflict the adult had with a younger sibling, cousin, or neighbor. The student and the adult should also talk about how the conflict was resolved. Volunteers can then share these stories with classmates.

34

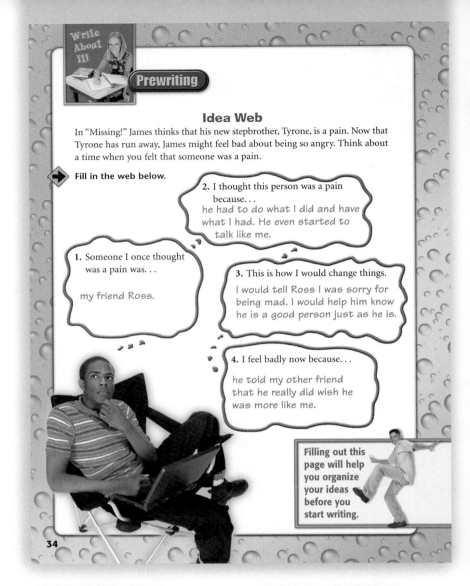

Prewriting

Idea Web

In "Missing!" James thinks that his new stepbrother, Tyrone, is a pain. Now that Tyrone has run away, James might feel bad about being so angry. Think about a time when you felt that someone was a pain.

➡ **Fill in the web below.**

1. Someone I once thought was a pain was. . .

my friend Ross.

2. I thought this person was a pain because. . .
he had to do what I did and have what I had. He even started to talk like me.

3. This is how I would change things.
I would tell Ross I was sorry for being mad. I would help him know he is a good person just as he is.

4. I feel badly now because. . .
he told my other friend that he really did wish he was more like me.

Filling out this page will help you organize your ideas before you start writing.

34

Before Writing

Have students brainstorm experiences they have had with people whom they thought were annoying and whom they regret treating badly. Have students write about these experiences in journals. If students are having trouble generating ideas, share with them a story from your own life. Reassure students that we all have conflicts with others and most of us have some regrets about these conflicts.

Or, have students work in small groups to brainstorm ideas before they begin working independently on their graphic organizers.

During Writing

Have students refer to their graphic organizers. Personalize the experience for students having difficulty. **Say,** *What happened with this person that made you think he or she was a pain? How do you wish things were different now?*

After Writing

Discuss students' reactions to what they have written. Encourage students to discuss the lessons they have learned about how to treat others.

Saying You're Sorry

A friendly letter is a good way to tell someone how you feel. It is written to someone you know fairly well. It has all the parts below.

➡ **Write a plan for a letter to say you are sorry to someone who upset you. Use ideas from your web.**

Date	October 23, 2003
Greeting	Dear ___Ross,___ ,
First paragraph: Tell how you feel and why.	I am writing to let you know that I feel ___angry.___ . I feel this way because ___I don't like that you do what I do.___
Second paragraph: Tell that you feel bad and that you are sorry.	I feel bad about how I feel because ___I know that you don't___ try to make me angry. I should feel glad that you want to be like me. ___. I am sorry.___
Third paragraph: Tell what changes you will make.	I want things to be better. The changes I would like to make are ___helping you know you are important and being your friend.___
Closing	Your friend, Lewis
Signature: Sign your name.	

Writing

➡ Write a letter telling someone that you are sorry. Use the plan above to help explain how you feel. You can add more sentences, but keep your ideas in the same order. Write your letter on another sheet of paper.

35

GROUP SHARING

When students have finished writing, organize them into pairs. Have each pair develop a list of ways to avoid having to apologize to others. Have volunteer pairs share their lists with the class. As a class, have students create a list of what they learned about how to treat people better.

Assessment

Portfolio Assessment
Students may want to save their letters in their classroom portfolios.

Student Self-Assessment
Encourage students to think about their writing experience. Say, *How did writing help you realize how much you care about this person? How do you think you can avoid having to say you are sorry to people later?*

SCORING RUBRIC: LETTER

SCORE 3

Letter fulfills purpose. Topic is clearly defined and supporting details are well developed. Contains clear, vivid sensory details. Writing is organized and coherent. Contains few errors in sentence structure, usage, mechanics, or spelling.

SCORE 2

Letter fulfills purpose. Topic is defined and supporting ideas are developed. Contains sensory details, but some are not vivid; some may not be clear. Has some degree of organization and coherence. Contains some errors in sentence structure, usage, mechanics, or spelling.

SCORE 1

Letter does not fulfill purpose. Topic is not defined and idea development is weak. Writing contains few or no sensory details and most are not vivid or clear. Has minimal organization and coherence. Contains many errors in sentence structure, usage, mechanics, or spelling.

Short i

Ask a volunteer to read aloud the rule about **short i.** Use *inch* as an example of a word that begins with the **short i** sound. Use the words *mitt* and *pig* as examples of when the **short i** comes in the middle of a word. Read the directions for the activity aloud. Discuss the first sentence. If students are having difficulty, read the sentence and the answer choices aloud, exaggerating the **short i** sound and reminding students that the answer should have an *i* sound that rhymes with *mitt, inch,* and *pig.* Have students complete the second sentence independently.

Long i

Ask a volunteer to read aloud the rule about **long i.** Use *ice* as an example of a word that begins with the **long i** sound. Use the words *time* and *light* as examples of when the **long i** comes in the middle of a word. Read the directions for the activity aloud. Discuss the third sentence. If students are having difficulty, read the sentence and answer choices aloud, exaggerating the **long i** sound and reminding students that the answer should have an *i* sound that rhymes with *ice, time,* and *light.* Have students complete the fourth sentence independently.

Have students complete sentences five through eight independently.

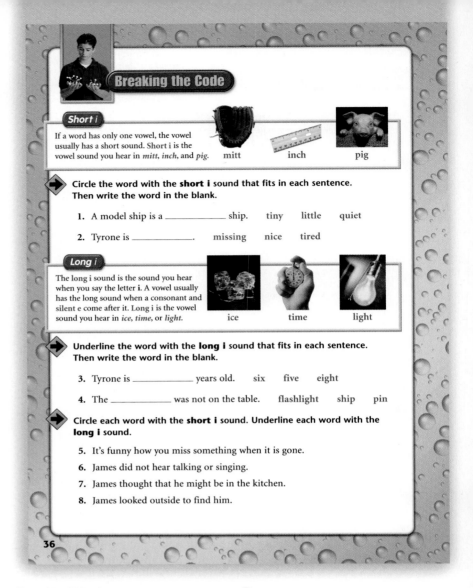

Breaking the Code

Short i

If a word has only one vowel, the vowel usually has a short sound. Short i is the vowel sound you hear in *mitt, inch,* and *pig.*   mitt   inch   pig

➡ Circle the word with the **short i** sound that fits in each sentence. Then write the word in the blank.

1. A model ship is a _____ ship.   tiny   little   quiet

2. Tyrone is _____.   missing   nice   tired

Long i

The long i sound is the sound you hear when you say the letter i. A vowel usually has the long sound when a consonant and silent e come after it. Long i is the vowel sound you hear in *ice, time,* or *light.*   ice   time   light

➡ Underline the word with the **long i** sound that fits in each sentence. Then write the word in the blank.

3. Tyrone is _____ years old.   six   five   eight

4. The _____ was not on the table.   flashlight   ship   pin

➡ Circle each word with the **short i** sound. Underline each word with the **long i** sound.

5. It's funny how you miss something when it is gone.

6. James did not hear talking or singing.

7. James thought that he might be in the kitchen.

8. James looked outside to find him.

36

Answers to Breaking the Code

1. (little)

2. (missing)

3. five

4. flashlight

5. (It's) (miss) (something) (it) (is)

6. (did) (talking) (singing)

7. might (in) (kitchen)

8. outside find (him)

RETEACHING

Group students in pairs. Have each pair generate a list of words with the **short i** and **long i** sounds that describe James or Tyrone. Have groups share their words, and list them on the board in two columns, **short i** and **long i.**

Then, have the pairs write short rhyming poems about James or Tyrone. Remind them to use rhyming words from the board in their poems.

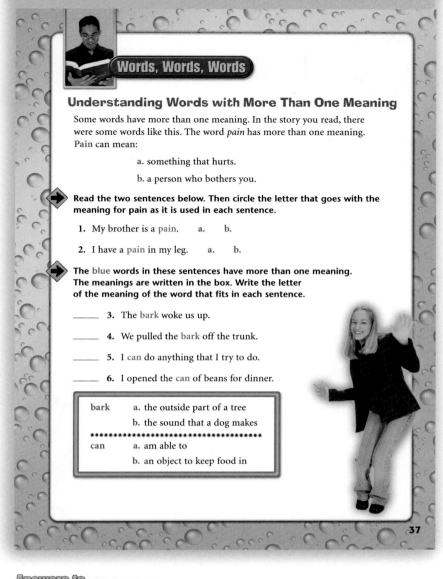

Words, Words, Words

Understanding Words with More Than One Meaning

Some words have more than one meaning. In the story you read, there were some words like this. The word *pain* has more than one meaning. Pain can mean:

a. something that hurts.

b. a person who bothers you.

Read the two sentences below. Then circle the letter that goes with the meaning for pain as it is used in each sentence.

1. My brother is a pain.　a.　b.

2. I have a pain in my leg.　a.　b.

The blue words in these sentences have more than one meaning. The meanings are written in the box. Write the letter of the meaning of the word that fits in each sentence.

_____ 3. The bark woke us up.

_____ 4. We pulled the bark off the trunk.

_____ 5. I can do anything that I try to do.

_____ 6. I opened the can of beans for dinner.

bark	a. the outside part of a tree
	b. the sound that a dog makes
can	a. am able to
	b. an object to keep food in

37

Answers to Words, Words, Words

1. **a person who bothers you   b**

2. **something that hurts   a**

3. **the sound that a dog makes   b**

4. **the outside part of a tree   a**

5. **am able to   a**

6. **an object to keep food in   b**

Words, Words, Words

Explain that some words are spelled and sound the same but have different meanings. The way to tell what meaning of the word was intended is to read or listen to the way the word is used.

Write the following two sentences on the board:

The students were in school.

The school of fish swam by.

Ask a volunteer to read the two sentences. **Ask,** *What are two different meanings for the word* school? Elicit from students that a school can be a building where children go to learn or it can be a group of fish. Ask students which words they used to determine which meaning of the word *school* was intended in each sentence.

Have students complete the Understanding Words with More Than One Meaning activity. Discuss what words helped them know which meaning of the word was intended in each sentence.

RETEACHING

Write the following sentences on the board:

After school, I head to baseball practice. I bring my bat, ball, and glove. When practice is over, I board the bus. I am ready to go back home.

Tell students that each of the underlined words has another meaning. Ask them to write new sentences that use each of the four words in another way.

REINFORCING THE THEME

To reinforce the theme, *Onward and Upward,* have students discuss explorers of new lands. Ask them to imagine what it was like for the first settlers in America. As a class, generate a list of words to describe the people who sailed halfway across the world to a new land. Then have students think of words to describe how those people must have felt when they arrived. Tell students the selection they will read is about a brave man who wanted to explore a different land.

STRATEGY FOCUS

Recognizing the sequence of events

Strategy

RECOGNIZING SEQUENCE

To understand the text, readers have to follow the sequence of events. Informational texts might follow chronological sequence or could be organized around a problem and solution, cause and effect, or comparison.

Historical events are often told in a chronological sequence. Readers should pay attention to clues such as the month or year of an event or words like *first, next, before, after,* or *later.*

The activities in this unit will help students apply the strategy of recognizing sequence.

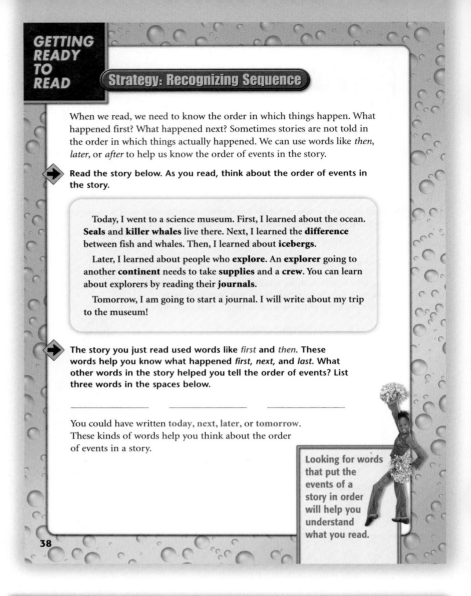

Strategy: Recognizing Sequence

When we read, we need to know the order in which things happen. What happened first? What happened next? Sometimes stories are not told in the order in which things actually happened. We can use words like *then, later,* or *after* to help us know the order of events in the story.

➡ Read the story below. As you read, think about the order of events in the story.

Today, I went to a science museum. First, I learned about the ocean. **Seals** and **killer whales** live there. Next, I learned the **difference** between fish and whales. Then, I learned about **icebergs**.

Later, I learned about people who **explore**. An **explorer** going to another **continent** needs to take **supplies** and a **crew**. You can learn about explorers by reading their **journals**.

Tomorrow, I am going to start a journal. I will write about my trip to the museum!

➡ The story you just read used words like *first* and *then*. These words help you know what happened *first, next,* and *last*. What other words in the story helped you tell the order of events? List three words in the spaces below.

_____   _____   _____

You could have written today, next, later, or tomorrow. These kinds of words help you think about the order of events in a story.

Looking for words that put the events of a story in order will help you understand what you read.

38

INTRODUCING THE STRATEGY

Have students read the story. Then have them complete the spaces for the three words independently or as a group. Ask students to share the words they wrote. Ask questions such as:

• How can words like *today, later,* or *tomorrow* help you decide the order of events?

• What was the sequence of events in this story?

Explain to students that recognizing sequence is important to understanding what they read.

Tell students they will use this strategy as they read the selection.

Note: The boldface words on this page are vocabulary words.

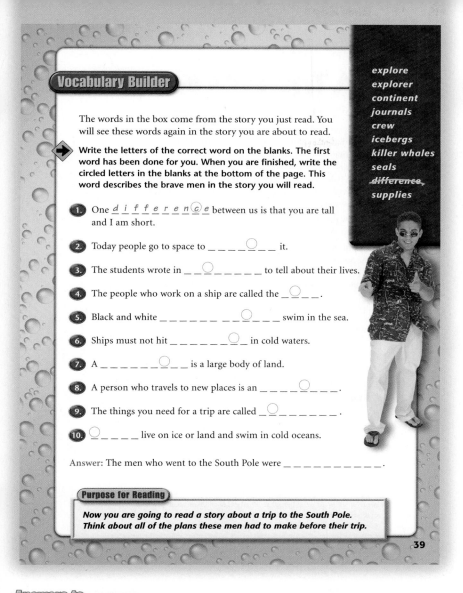

Vocabulary Builder

The words in the box come from the story you just read. You will see these words again in the story you are about to read.

explore
explorer
continent
journals
crew
icebergs
killer whales
seals
difference
supplies

➤ Write the letters of the correct word on the blanks. The first word has been done for you. When you are finished, write the circled letters in the blanks at the bottom of the page. This word describes the brave men in the story you will read.

1. One _d i f f e r e n (c) e_ between us is that you are tall and I am short.

2. Today people go to space to _ _ _ _ ◯ _ _ it.

3. The students wrote in _ _ ◯ _ _ _ _ _ to tell about their lives.

4. The people who work on a ship are called the _ ◯ _ _.

5. Black and white _ _ _ _ _ _ _ _ ◯ _ _ swim in the sea.

6. Ships must not hit _ _ _ _ _ _ ◯ in cold waters.

7. A _ _ _ _ _ _ ◯ _ _ is a large body of land.

8. A person who travels to new places is an _ _ _ _ ◯ _ _ _.

9. The things you need for a trip are called _ ◯ _ _ _ _ _ _.

10. ◯ _ _ _ live on ice or land and swim in cold oceans.

Answer: The men who went to the South Pole were _ _ _ _ _ _ _ _ _ _.

Purpose for Reading

Now you are going to read a story about a trip to the South Pole. Think about all of the plans these men had to make before their trip.

39

Vocabulary Builder

This activity introduces vocabulary words from the selection students will read. Completing the activity will help students understand these words in the selection. For additional reinforcement, the vocabulary words are defined in footnotes throughout the selection.

Assessment

Check students' comprehension by having them write their own definitions for each word.

- **continent**
- **crew**
- **difference**
- **explore**
- **explorer**
- **icebergs**
- **journals**
- **killer whales**
- **seals**
- **supplies**

Answers to Vocabulary Builder

1. **The first answer is provided for students. differen(c)e**

2. expl(o)re

3. jo(u)rnals

4. c(r)ew

5. killer wh(a)les

6. iceber(g)s

7. contin(e)nt

8. expl(o)rer

9. s(u)pplies

10. (s)eals

The men who went to the South Pole were (courageous).

VOCABULARY EXTENSION

Organize students into small groups. Give each group a paper with a vocabulary word written in the center. Have students create word concept maps by drawing lines out from the vocabulary word in the center. At the end of each line, have them write a related word. Tell students the related words can be other words from the vocabulary list or any words. Have groups share their maps with the class, explaining why they chose the related words they did.

A Trip to the Bottom of the World

SELECTION AT A GLANCE

This selection describes the preparations that Ernest Shackleton made for his incredible 1914 attempt to cross the South Pole.

INTERESTING FACTS

The story of Shackleton's legendary expedition to the South Pole was made into a giant-screen film. A production team making the movie took two trips to the Antarctic during 1999 and 2000 where they retraced the journey of Shackleton's original crew during their 17-month ordeal.

A Trip to the Bottom of the World

Today, we **explore** space. A hundred years ago, we were still exploring new land on Earth. The South Pole had just been reached. This land was new to all people. No one had ever lived at the South Pole. No one had even gone there. It was too windy. Winds of up to 200 miles an hour blew across it. It was too cold. Ice covered the land. In some places the ice was two miles deep.

Few people wanted to go to the South Pole, but many people wanted to know about it. They sent people to explore it for them.

This is the amazing story of Sir Ernest Shackleton's third trip to the South Pole.

> 1. What did Shackleton do before he made this trip? Write what you think.

Another Trip

It was 1914, and Sir Ernest Shackleton was ready for another trip. Shackleton was an English **explorer.** He had been to the South Pole two times before, but he had not reached the point that is the real South Pole. He had to turn back because of bad weather. In 1912, another team was the first ever to reach the South Pole. Shackleton wanted to be first to cross it.

---

explore (ehk SPLAWR) *verb* To explore is to travel to and learn about new lands.
explorer (ehk SPLAWR uhr) *noun* An explorer is a person who travels to and learns about new lands.

40

Before Reading

INTRODUCING THE SELECTION

Have students think about the preparations they engage in when they get ready to go on a trip or just to school. Discuss these preparations. Then, have students brainstorm the preparations that would be required for a journey to the South Pole. Write students' ideas on the board. Remind students that Shackleton was traveling in 1914, so he did not have access to the modern technology that explorers would have today.

During Reading

PURPOSE FOR READING

Students read to find out how Shackleton prepared for his journey.

APPLYING THE STRATEGY

Have students read the selection "A Trip to the Bottom of the World." Remind students that they will answer Think-Along questions while they read the selection, and that answering these questions will help them think about the sequence of events.

Possible Responses

Question 1

If I were him I would buy warm clothes.

This response shows the student is connecting personally with the text. Say, *He probably did because it would be so cold. What else would you do to prepare?*

Why would people go there?

Responding with a question is a common response. This shows the student is thinking about what has been read. Say, *What in the story gives you clues about why Shackleton wanted to go?*

The land at the South Pole is called Antarctica. It is a **continent** covered by ice that is four to six feet deep in most places. The trip would be long and hard, but Shackleton was ready to go again.

Paying for the Trip

The trip to Antarctica would cost a lot of money. Shackleton knew some important people. He was well known because of his other trips. Many people agreed to help pay for the trip.

Shackleton also planned to make money. During the trip, his team would take pictures. The men would write in **journals.** Shackleton would sell the story of the trip when he returned.

2. What do you think were the first things the men wrote in their journals?

Sir Ernest Shackleton planned his third trip to the South Pole in 1914.

___

continent (KAHNT ihn uhnt) *noun* A continent is a very large piece of land on Earth.
journals (JUR nuhlz) *noun* Journals are blank books that people write their thoughts in.

Question 2

They probably told about themselves.

This student makes a logical conclusion, perhaps based on experience writing in a journal. **Say,** *Why do you think they might tell about themselves?*

Stuff about the trip

This simple response shows comprehension of the text. Encourage this student to connect with the text. **Say,** *What kind of information would you like to read in a journal about a trip to the South Pole?*

Strategy Tip

As students read, encourage them to think about the sequence of events in the selection by listing the steps that Shackleton took to prepare for his journey.

NONFICTION READING STRATEGY

Table of Contents

Ask for a volunteer to explain what a table of contents is. Looking at the table of contents before reading can help readers predict what they will learn and see how the text is sequenced.

Explain that this selection is a chapter from a longer book called *Danger on Ice.* Tell students that this book has the following chapters:

Have students write short predictions about the contents of each chapter of the book.

Repeat the activity with other books students are reading.

✓ Making Travel Plans

Shackleton began planning his trip. His ship would travel south from England, then his team would walk across Antarctica. A second ship would sail south from Australia to Antarctica. This ship would pick up Shackleton's men and return them to England.

✓ Getting Ready

Shackleton had a few months to get ready. First, he bought two strong wooden ships. He named one ship *Endurance*. Endurance is the strength to keep going when things are hard. This was the ship that Shackleton and his team would use to get to Antarctica. The second ship, *Aurora*, would bring them home.

Next, Shackleton needed to choose a good **crew.** The men of the *Endurance* had to be strong. They would have to live through storms with ice, snow, and wind. They would see huge **icebergs** that could break a ship to pieces. They could fall through ice into the water. Under the ice, **killer whales** swam. The killer whales ate **seals.** From under the ice, a man would look like a seal.

---

crew (KROO) *noun* A crew is the people who work on a ship.
icebergs (YS burgz) *noun* Icebergs are huge chunks of ice that float in cold seas.
killer whales (KIHL uhr WAYLZ) *noun* Killer whales are very large black and white animals that live in the ocean and eat fish and seals.
seals (SEELZ) *noun* Seals are animals with smooth skins that live in cold oceans.

42

Notes

3. Why do you think Shackleton needed strong ships?

Shackleton was so well known that 5,000 people wanted to join his crew. Shackleton knew that he had to choose carefully. The right crew could mean the **difference** between life and death.

First, Shackleton chose men he knew from his other trips. Frank Wild would be second in charge. Tom Crean would be second officer. Frank Worsley would be the captain.

Next, Shackleton chose artists. The artists would draw, paint, and take pictures of Antarctica.

Then, Shackleton found a cook, doctors, and some scientists. The scientists would study the ice and the shape of Antarctica. They would also study the animals and weather.

The crew gets the *Endurance* ready for the long trip.

---

difference (DIHF uhr uhns) *noun* Difference is the way in which things are not alike.

43

RECIPROCAL TEACHING

Predict

Encourage students to make predictions as they read.

When students finish reading the selection, write the last two lines on the board: *Shackleton bought enough supplies for two years. He knew that it was best to be safe.* Ask students to make predictions about what they think will happen on the trip. Encourage students to support these predictions with information from the selection or with background knowledge.

Question 3

There would be storms and ice.

This response demonstrates a careful reader. The student makes a connection between the paragraph on the ships and the paragraph on the types of men needed for the crew.

If they didn't have strong ships, they might die.

This student makes an inference and shows an understanding of the cause and effect relationship between having strong ships and a safe journey.

It is very important to have students read and discuss the selection and their responses to the Think-Along questions in the boxes.

DISCUSSING THE RESPONSES

- Ask for at least three different responses to each question to emphasize the many possible responses. **Say,** *That was one good response. Did anyone else have a different response?*

- Share your own responses. Explain what features from the text made you write what you did.

RETEACHING

Have groups of three to five students work together to write a brief summary of what they have read. Prompt students to plan their summaries by thinking about the main ideas of the selection and by thinking about what happened first, next, and last.

Have different groups share their summaries with the class and discuss what different details each group chose to include in its summary.

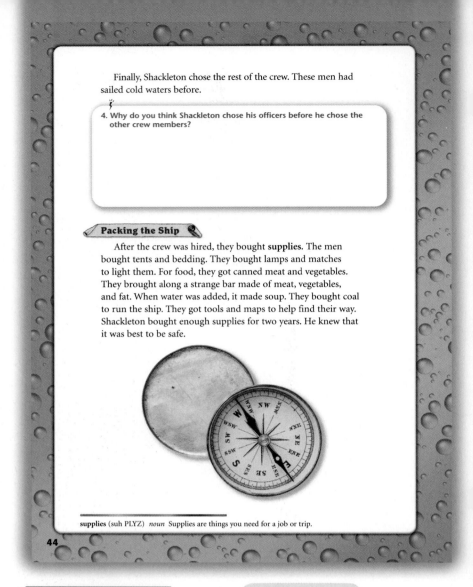

Finally, Shackleton chose the rest of the crew. These men had sailed cold waters before.

4. Why do you think Shackleton chose his officers before he chose the other crew members?

Packing the Ship

After the crew was hired, they bought **supplies.** The men bought tents and bedding. They bought lamps and matches to light them. For food, they got canned meat and vegetables. They brought along a strange bar made of meat, vegetables, and fat. When water was added, it made soup. They bought coal to run the ship. They got tools and maps to help find their way. Shackleton bought enough supplies for two years. He knew that it was best to be safe.

supplies (suh PLYZ) *noun* Supplies are things you need for a job or trip.

44

Informal Assessment
To assess students' comprehension, use their written responses and oral discussion.

Student Self-Assessment
Encourage students to evaluate their own comprehension by responding to this question: *Was it easy or difficult for you to understand this selection? Explain why.*

Possible Responses

Question 4

The crew should decide.

It is not clear from this response whether the student misunderstood the text or is making a judgment about the sequence Shackleton used to select his crew. **Ask,** *Did Shackleton think the crew should decide who would lead? What makes you think so?*

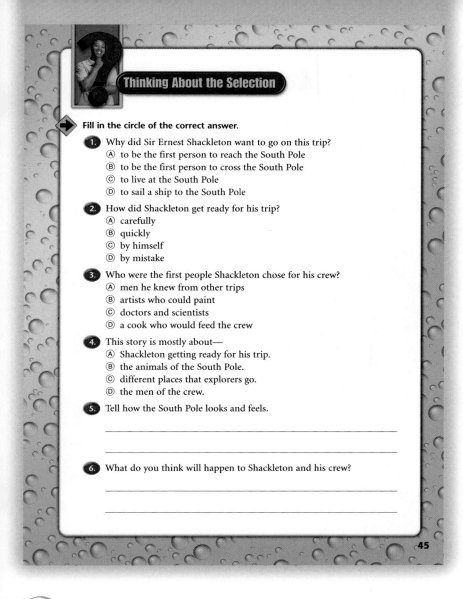

Thinking About the Selection

Fill in the circle of the correct answer.

1. Why did Sir Ernest Shackleton want to go on this trip?
   - Ⓐ to be the first person to reach the South Pole
   - Ⓑ to be the first person to cross the South Pole
   - Ⓒ to live at the South Pole
   - Ⓓ to sail a ship to the South Pole

2. How did Shackleton get ready for his trip?
   - Ⓐ carefully
   - Ⓑ quickly
   - Ⓒ by himself
   - Ⓓ by mistake

3. Who were the first people Shackleton chose for his crew?
   - Ⓐ men he knew from other trips
   - Ⓑ artists who could paint
   - Ⓒ doctors and scientists
   - Ⓓ a cook who would feed the crew

4. This story is mostly about—
   - Ⓐ Shackleton getting ready for his trip.
   - Ⓑ the animals of the South Pole.
   - Ⓒ different places that explorers go.
   - Ⓓ the men of the crew.

5. Tell how the South Pole looks and feels.

   _____

   _____

6. What do you think will happen to Shackleton and his crew?

   _____

   _____

45

It is easier if you know who is in charge.

This response shows comprehension. Encourage elaboration. Ask, *How is it easier if you know who is in charge?*

Thinking About the Selection

Explain that answering these questions will help students check their comprehension. Answering these questions will also help them practice for other reading tests.

Have students answer the questions. Explain that, as on other tests, each multiple-choice question has one right answer, but the last two questions can be answered in different ways.

Answers to Thinking About the Selection

1. **B. to be the first person to cross the South Pole** (Literal—Main Idea)
2. **A. carefully** (Inferential—Summarize)
3. **A. men he knew from other trips** (Literal—Sequence)
4. **A. Shackleton getting ready for his trip.** (Inferential—Main Idea)
5. Accept all reasonable responses, including: *It is white and gray because it is so icy and cold.* (Literal—Details)
6. Accept all reasonable responses, including: *They planned so carefully I think they will make it.* or *It is so dangerous and no one did it before so I think they will have problems.* (Inferential—Prediction)

45

READING LINKS

Students who enjoyed "A Trip to the Bottom of the World" might want to read the entire book, *Danger on Ice*. Students might enjoy reading other books about exploration and courageous journeys.

Reading Aloud

- *The Broken Blade* by William Durbin (Bantam Doubleday Dell, 1998). [F]
- *Buried in Ice: The Mystery of a Lost Arctic Expedition* by Owen Beattie (Scholastic, 1993). [NF]
- *Jacques Cousteau and the Undersea World* by Roger King (Chelsea House, 2000). [NF]
- *Reaching for the Moon: The Apollo Astronauts* by Hal Marcovitz (Chelsea House, 2000). [NF]

Independent Reading

- *Amelia Earhart: Pioneer of the Sky* by John Parlin (Dell, 1991). [NF]
- *Vikings* by Stewart Ross (Millbrook, 2000). [NF]
- *Sacagawea* by Jan Gleiter (Steck-Vaughn, 1998). [NF]

FAMILY INVOLVEMENT

Ask each student to bring from home a souvenir or symbol of a trip or experience with his or her family. Have students ask family members about their memories of the experience. Volunteers can share stories with the class.

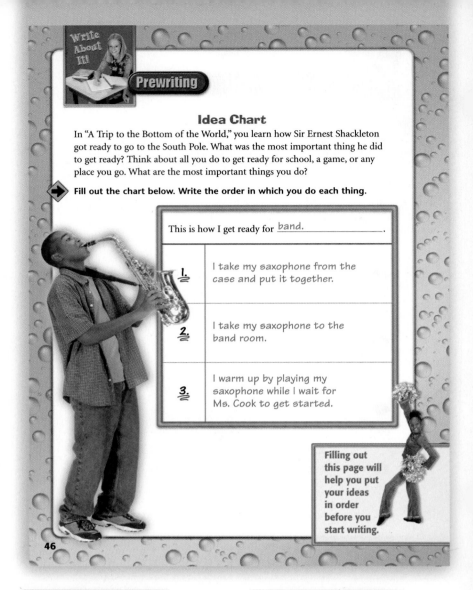

Prewriting

Idea Chart

In "A Trip to the Bottom of the World," you learn how Sir Ernest Shackleton got ready to go to the South Pole. What was the most important thing he did to get ready? Think about all you do to get ready for school, a game, or any place you go. What are the most important things you do?

➡ **Fill out the chart below. Write the order in which you do each thing.**

This is how I get ready for <u>band.</u>

1.	I take my saxophone from the case and put it together.
2.	I take my saxophone to the band room.
3.	I warm up by playing my saxophone while I wait for Ms. Cook to get started.

Filling out this page will help you put your ideas in order before you start writing.

Before Writing

Have students brainstorm a list of the activities they do regularly. Ask some students to tell what they do to get ready for one activity. If students are having trouble generating ideas, provide some examples of things that you do and how you get ready.

Or, have students work in small groups to brainstorm ideas before they begin working independently on their charts.

During Writing

Refer students to their charts. Personalize the experience for students having difficulty. Say, *How would you tell a friend who didn't have a lot of time what you need to do to get ready for something? What are the steps that you have to take?*

After Writing

As a group, discuss students' reactions to what they have written. Ask students whether writing their summaries helped them think about what they do to get ready.

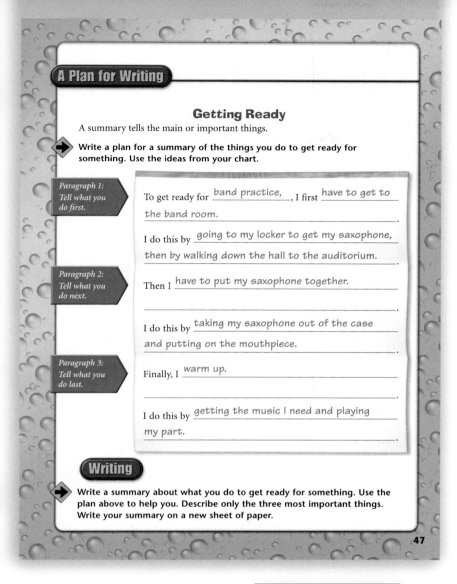

A Plan for Writing

Getting Ready

A summary tells the main or important things.

➤ Write a plan for a summary of the things you do to get ready for something. Use the ideas from your chart.

Paragraph 1:
Tell what you do first.

To get ready for _band practice,_ I first _have to get to the band room._

I do this by _going to my locker to get my saxophone, then by walking down the hall to the auditorium._

Paragraph 2:
Tell what you do next.

Then I _have to put my saxophone together._

I do this by _taking my saxophone out of the case and putting on the mouthpiece._

Paragraph 3:
Tell what you do last.

Finally, I _warm up._

I do this by _getting the music I need and playing my part._

Writing

➤ Write a summary about what you do to get ready for something. Use the plan above to help you. Describe only the three most important things. Write your summary on a new sheet of paper.

47

GROUP SHARING

Organize students into groups of four or five when they have finished writing. Have each group select the shortest summary and the clearest summary from the group. Ask groups whether the shortest and clearest are the same. Have each group summarize the selection process for the rest of the class.

Assessment

Portfolio Assessment
Students may want to save their summaries in their classroom portfolios.

Student Self-Assessment
Encourage students to think about their writing experience. **Say,** *Why is it important to summarize information? How often do you think you give people summaries of events, movies, television shows, or experiences without even knowing that you are?*

SCORING RUBRIC: SUMMARY

SCORE 3
Summary contains no extraneous information. Topic is clearly defined and supporting details are well developed. Writing is clear, organized, and coherent. Contains few errors in sentence structure, usage, mechanics, or spelling.

SCORE 2
Summary contains little extraneous information. Topic is defined and supporting ideas are developed. Writing shows some degree of organization and coherence, but may be unclear in places. Contains some errors in sentence structure, usage, mechanics, or spelling.

SCORE 1
Summary contains extraneous information or does not adhere to topic. Topic is not clearly defined or idea development is weak. Writing is not clear. Has minimal organization and coherence. Contains many errors in sentence structure, usage, mechanics, or spelling.

Breaking the Code

Short o

Ask a volunteer to read aloud the rule about **short o.** Point out that all of the **short o** examples—*dog, mop, box*—have only one vowel.

Read the directions for the activity aloud. Discuss the first sentence. If students are having difficulty, read the sentence and answer choices aloud, exaggerating the **short o** sound and reminding students that the answer should have an *o* sound that rhymes with *dog, mop,* and *box.* Have students complete the second sentence independently.

Long o

Ask a volunteer to read aloud the rule about **long o.** Use *goat* as an example of a word that has two vowels together and makes a **long o** sound. Use the words *home* and *rose* as examples of when the **long o** sound is made by a silent *e.*

Read the directions for the activity aloud. Discuss the third sentence. If students are having difficulty, read the sentence and answer choices aloud, exaggerating the **long o** sound and reminding students that the answer should have an *o* sound that rhymes with *goat, home,* and *rose.* Have students complete the fourth sentence independently.

Have students complete sentences five through eight independently.

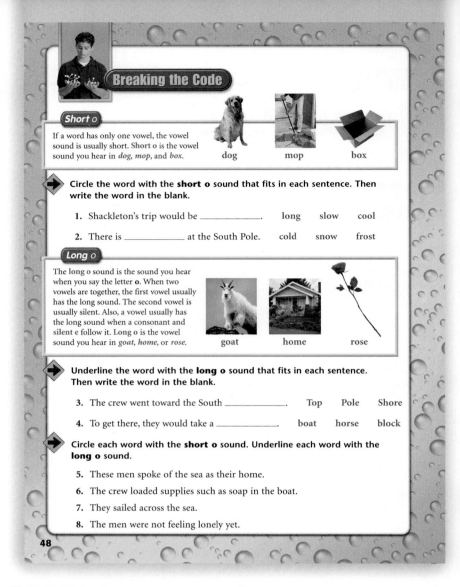

Breaking the Code

Short o

If a word has only one vowel, the vowel sound is usually short. Short o is the vowel sound you hear in *dog, mop,* and *box.*

dog   mop   box

Circle the word with the **short o** sound that fits in each sentence. Then write the word in the blank.

1. Shackleton's trip would be _____.   long   slow   cool

2. There is _____ at the South Pole.   cold   snow   frost

Long o

The long o sound is the sound you hear when you say the letter **o.** When two vowels are together, the first vowel usually has the long sound. The second vowel is usually silent. Also, a vowel usually has the long sound when a consonant and silent e follow it. Long o is the vowel sound you hear in *goat, home,* or *rose.*

goat   home   rose

Underline the word with the **long o** sound that fits in each sentence. Then write the word in the blank.

3. The crew went toward the South _____.   Top   Pole   Shore

4. To get there, they would take a _____.   boat   horse   block

Circle each word with the **short o** sound. Underline each word with the **long o** sound.

5. These men spoke of the sea as their home.

6. The crew loaded supplies such as soap in the boat.

7. They sailed across the sea.

8. The men were not feeling lonely yet.

48

Answers to Breaking the Code

1. (long)

2. (frost)

3. Pole

4. boat

5. spoke (of) home

6. loaded   soap   boat

7. (across)

8. (not) lonely

RETEACHING

Divide the class in half. Have one group look through the selection to find as many **short o** words as they can. Have the other group find as many **long o** words as they can.

Write both lists on the board. Discuss whether the class can make any generalizations about the lists, such as that there are more words with one *o* sound than the other.

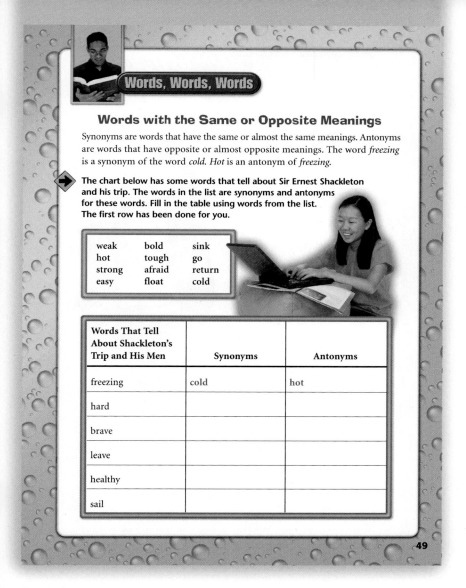

Words with the Same or Opposite Meanings

Synonyms are words that have the same or almost the same meanings. Antonyms are words that have opposite or almost opposite meanings. The word *freezing* is a synonym of the word *cold*. *Hot* is an antonym of *freezing*.

The chart below has some words that tell about Sir Ernest Shackleton and his trip. The words in the list are synonyms and antonyms for these words. Fill in the table using words from the list. The first row has been done for you.

weak	bold	sink
hot	tough	go
strong	afraid	return
easy	float	cold

Words That Tell About Shackleton's Trip and His Men	Synonyms	Antonyms
freezing	cold	hot
hard		
brave		
leave		
healthy		
sail		

49

Shackleton sailed the <u>sea</u>.

His trip was to be a <u>short</u> one.

Ask a volunteer to read the two sentences. **Ask,** *Which of these sentences is true?* Elicit from students that the first is true but the second is false. Explain that substituting synonyms for words in sentences keeps the meaning the same but an antonym changes the meaning. Ask students to supply a synonym for *sea* that would keep the meaning of the sentence true. Ask students to supply an antonym for *short* that would make the second sentence true.

Have students complete the Words with the Same or Opposite Meanings activity. Discuss whether students found the activity difficult to complete.

Answers to Words, Words, Words

Words That Tell About Shackleton's Trip and His Men	Synonyms	Antonyms
freezing	cold	hot
hard	tough	easy
brave	bold	afraid
leave	go	return
healthy	strong	weak
sail	float	sink

RETEACHING

Group students into pairs. Have each student write a brief description of a person or place. Then have the two students switch descriptions and rewrite each description using as many synonyms or as many antonyms as they can. Have them return the description to the original writer and have that writer identify whether the rewrite included synonyms or antonyms.

THEME WRAP-UP SELECTIONS

There are two types of selections in this Theme Wrap-Up. The first selection is a fiction story and the second selection is a nonfiction article. These selections serve three purposes.

First, they offer another perspective on the theme *Onward and Upward* that can be used as a basis for discussion. After your students have finished reading, you may want to engage them in a discussion or writing activity about how these selections fit into the theme *Onward and Upward*.

Second, the selections provide another venue for using Think-Along questions and practicing some of the strategies taught in this theme. These selections are designed to show students how thinking along will help them comprehend what they are reading and better answer questions about what they have read.

Third, the selections provide models similar to reading comprehension passages on standardized tests. Each selection is followed by a set of multiple-choice and short-answer questions. The question format is typical of many standardized and criterion-referenced tests. These questions help students check comprehension and prepare them for taking standardized tests.

I DON'T WANT TO GO!

During the summer before my seventh-grade school year, my dad told us we were moving from Omaha, Nebraska, to Santa Cruz, California. At first I was sad, but then I got so mad that I decided to stop talking.

Mom told me that I was only thinking of myself. She said that Dad felt bad enough about moving us so far away. I was just making things worse. Then she said the most terrible thing. "Samantha, why can't you act more like Merri and Heather? They are looking forward to meeting new friends."

How could she do that? It wasn't fair, because I knew my sisters felt the same way I did. Merri and Heather just knew how to look happy when anyone was watching.

1. How do you think Samantha will feel when she gets to her new home? Why do you think that?

50

PURPOSE FOR READING

Tell students they will read the selection and answer the questions that follow so they can get more practice using the reading strategies they have learned.

Possible Responses

Question 1

I think she will like it because she will get to be near the beach in California.

This student makes a personal connection with the story. **Ask,** *What in the story makes you think she will like it?*

She'll be unhappy because she already is really mad.

This student makes a prediction based on textual evidence so far.

My being unhappy did nothing to stop the men from coming and moving all of our stuff into a big truck. The driver told my dad he would meet us at the new house on Friday. Then he drove away with almost everything we owned.

We got into the family van and headed to my grandma and grandpa's farm. We got there in about an hour. It seemed to take almost that long to take all the suitcases inside. We put some of our things in the extra bedroom and the rest of it in the corner of the den.

After dinner, my sisters and I washed dishes. I complained about having to do dishes, but Merri and Heather told me to hush. They wanted to hear what the adults were saying in the other room.

Dad talked about the new job. He said that it was going to be a big change but a good change. He told about finding the ad in the newspaper. He felt lucky that the ad had been placed in the Omaha paper. I didn't know how Dad felt about the new job. I almost felt bad for making him feel bad.

Then they turned to the subject I hate most. "Oh, how the girls are changing," Grandma said. "Merri gets more beautiful every day."

2. Why do you think Samantha hates the subject of the girls changing?

Grandpa talked about how smart Heather is. He said, "Heather will go far. She asks such good questions, and she knows so much for her age."

I was not so lucky. Grandma and Grandpa decided to talk about how tall I was getting. They always do. Grandma asked, "Where do you find jeans long enough for Samantha's legs?"

51

Question 2

Maybe it is the same thing they always talk about.

This student's response goes beyond the text and shows that the student is thinking carefully about what is read. Ask, *What makes you think it is the same thing they always talk about?*

Because they say the other girls are pretty and smart and she is just tall.

This student has read ahead to answer this question. Reading ahead is an effective reading strategy in this situation. Ask, *Why do you think Samantha wouldn't like this?*

Mom answered, "I can still fit her in boy's extra long jeans. After she begins to fill out, I don't know what we will do."

From the kitchen, I yelled, "Mom! Please!" But she didn't know what I was upset about. Merri just looked at me with that "I pity you" look on her face. Heather laughed and asked, "How is the weather up there?" I don't think she's so clever.

We spent the night at Grandma and Grandpa's. The next morning, we had a big breakfast. Then it was time to leave. Everyone acted like they weren't crying.

I tried to keep quiet, but I couldn't do it. I yelled, "I don't want to go!" Everyone just stared at me. I went on, "If you're all so sad, why are we going?"

Mom said, "That's enough, Samantha." She told me to get in the van. Everyone hugged one another, and we drove away.

Two very long days later, we got to a hotel in Santa Cruz. I slept most of the way, until Heather yelled at me to wake up. It was time to carry my suitcase to the room. Then I went back to sleep inside.

The next morning, we were in a hurry to go outside. The last two hours of our drive had been in the dark, so we didn't know what Santa Cruz looked like.

For July, it was cool outside. Even Merri and Heather said it was too cold.

3. How do you think Samantha feels about Santa Cruz now? Why do you think that?

Dad drove us down to the ocean. We walked along the beach. I saved some pretty seashells. We ate lunch at a place that looked over the bay. I loved being near the ocean.

52

Possible Responses

Question 3

She probably wishes it were warmer.

Encourage this student to think beyond this literal answer. **Ask,** *How else do you think Samantha is feeling about her move?*

She hasn't had enough time. I think she will start to like it. This student makes a prediction based on background knowledge and story details. **Ask,** *What makes you think so?*

After lunch, Dad drove us through a neighborhood of beautiful old homes. The trees were large, the grass was green, and many of the houses had big porches.

Finally, it was time to go see our new neighborhood. The house was small, but I would finally have a room to myself. I have always wanted my own room. Mom told me that the blue room was mine. She knew that I would need plenty of room for all my books.

We went back to the hotel to spend another night. Early the next morning, we checked out of the hotel. Then we went back to the house to meet the movers.

The men who helped us move came with our things and took everything out of the truck. There were boxes everywhere. What a mess! It took several days of hard work for us to put everything in its place.

The neighbors were friendly. I even made a new friend, Anna. She is my age. She is also the first friend I have had who is as tall as I am. We laughed together at all the tall jokes we have heard. Anna moved here two years ago from El Paso, Texas. She said she felt just the way I did, but now she really likes it!

I didn't want to move to Santa Cruz, but everything seems to be working out just fine. I don't think I'll say that to my parents just yet, though.

4. Why do you think Samantha doesn't want to tell her parents how she feels?

Question 4

It's hard to admit you were wrong.

This response is based on background knowledge and textual evidence. **Ask,** *What makes you think so?*

She was wrong.
Encourage this student to expand upon this response. **Ask,** *Why do you think that would make it hard for her to tell her parents?*

Explain that answering these questions will help students check their comprehension. Answering these questions will also help them practice for other reading tests.

Have students answer the questions. Explain that, as on other tests, each multiple-choice question has one right answer, but the last question can have more than one correct answer.

Answers to Theme Wrap-Up

1. **A. how one girl feels about her family moving** (Inferential—Main Idea)
2. **D. Samantha's father has a new job.** (Literal—Supporting Details)
3. **A. her father will change his mind.** (Inferential—Making Inferences)
4. **D. Samantha stops talking.** (Literal—Sequence)
5. **C. grumbled.** (Inferential—Vocabulary)
6. Accept all reasonable responses, including: *She has her own room and she met a new friend who is tall like she is.* (Literal—Supporting Details)

ONWARD AND UPWARD *Wrap-Up*

➤ **Fill in the circle of the correct answer.**

1. What is this story mostly about?
   - Ⓐ how one girl feels about her family moving
   - Ⓑ how Santa Cruz and Omaha are different
   - Ⓒ what it is like growing up with sisters
   - Ⓓ different reasons people move

2. Why is Samantha's family moving?
   - Ⓐ They need a bigger house.
   - Ⓑ They want to live closer to their family.
   - Ⓒ Samantha's sisters want to go to a new high school.
   - Ⓓ Samantha's father has a new job.

3. At the beginning of the story, Samantha hopes that—
   - Ⓐ her father will change his mind.
   - Ⓑ her sisters will tell her how they feel about moving.
   - Ⓒ she can stay at her grandma's house.
   - Ⓓ she can have a different teacher.

4. Which of these events happens first in the story?
   - Ⓐ Samantha's family goes to the ocean.
   - Ⓑ Samantha's family spends the night in a hotel.
   - Ⓒ Samantha's family spends the night at her grandma's house.
   - Ⓓ Samantha stops talking.

5. The word **complained** in this story is another word for—
   - Ⓐ agreed.
   - Ⓑ laughed.
   - Ⓒ grumbled.
   - Ⓓ hurried.

6. Describe two reasons Samantha likes her new home.

   _____

   _____

54

Notes

From Ice to Scream

Life becomes a short, thrilling ride when you get on a roller coaster. You can race along at speeds up to 100 miles an hour. You get turned upside down and spun around. You dive straight down.

Your heart and stomach seem to trade places. You scream as your hair stands on end. At the ride's end, you climb off the coaster. You can walk away on shaking legs or get back in line.

> 1. How might you feel after riding on a roller coaster?

The first roller coasters were made in Russia in the 1600s. They were ice slides. The tracks were cut tree trunks that workers sprayed with water. Ice formed because it was so cold. The sleds were huge ice blocks with straw stuffed in cut-out holes. People climbed a 70-foot ladder to take a ride. They got into an ice block, sat on the straw pad, and held on to a rope. Sand slowed the sled at the end of the ride. At speeds up to 50 miles an hour, the ride lasted only a few seconds.

55

PURPOSE FOR READING

Tell students they will read the selection and answer the questions that follow so they can get more practice using the reading strategies they have learned.

Question 1

I'd feel like doing it again.

I think I would want to throw up.

Both of these responses make the kinds of personal connections that this question elicits. Encourage students to share their experiences with roller coasters. **Ask,** *Have you ridden on a roller coaster before? What was it like?*

A man tried to build an ice slide in France. The ice melted because the weather was too warm, but he did not give up. He built a wooden hill with rollers in the middle of the track. He put runners on the bottom of the wooden sleds. The sleds went down the rollers. The name "roller coaster" started with this invention.

Another important change in coasters came from France. Tracks took the place of the rollers. They used small cars with wheels instead of sleds. The cars did not always stay on the tracks, and accidents often happened.

Other inventors worked to make roller coasters better and faster. Someone decided to turn riders upside down. The first circle shape on a roller coaster came to France in 1846. They tested and tested the **loop** before people could get on it. They used bags of sand, monkeys, flowers, eggs, and glasses of water as riders. These loops did not last long because they were too hard on people.

The first true roller coaster built in the United States was built at Coney Island in 1884. Coney Island was a beach and a park in New York. This coaster moved over wooden waves. It cost a nickel to ride. The coaster moved at six miles an hour. People enjoyed the ride. In just three weeks, the builder had earned back his $1,600 cost.

2. Why do you think the first roller coaster at Coney Island was so popular?

Possible Responses

Question 2

It was probably popular because it was fun and only a nickel.

This student makes an interpretation: anything fun that costs a nickel would be popular. Ask, *Why do you think it would be popular because of how much it costs?*

People might not have had a lot to do.

This student uses background knowledge. Ask, *What makes you think this would make them like roller coasters?*

In the 1920s people liked wooden roller coasters, such as the Cyclone. The Cyclone was named after a strong wind that blows around and around. Ads said that the Cyclone was the most frightening coaster ever built.

The ads did not scare riders away. On the first day, 75,000 people rode the Cyclone on Coney Island.

By 1929, there were more than 1,500 roller coasters in the United States. Some of these wooden coasters still run today.

> 3. What do you think will be the next big change in roller coasters? Why do you think so?

In the 1930s and the 1940s, the United States went through hard times. Not many people had money to go to parks with rides. The owners could not keep the coasters in good shape. They could not get new parts because of World War II. Soon there were only about two hundred coasters left in the United States.

In 1955 Walt Disney built a new park in California. His Matterhorn ride was the first roller coaster built on steel tracks. The ride went high in the air just like the Matterhorn mountain. These new tracks added twists, turns, and thrills to the ride. Not many parks built coasters in the 1960s and 1970s.

By 1980, roller coasters had changed. Some of the new ones had cars hanging down from the tracks. The cars could swing to the side. Bars across laps and over shoulders held riders in place.

The first coaster of this kind was the Bat. Cars in the shape of bats gave riders a feeling of flying. High costs to fix the Bat caused it to shut down in 1984.

57

Question 3

It will make you do different things like hang upside down or feel like you are in space.

This student is making a prediction about what will come next in the history of roller coasters. The response may be based on the student's own experiences. **Ask,** *What makes you think so?*

It will be more like virtual reality where you feel like you are somewhere else.

This response makes a prediction based on background knowledge of virtual-reality simulators. **Ask,** *What makes you think so?*

That same year the Big Bad Wolf opened in Virginia. It was a great ride for those who were not afraid. It swung the riders from right to left. Two water jets sprayed their faces. As the ride ended, the riders heard the cry of a big bad wolf.

Next came a roller coaster on which riders could stand up. The first of these was the King Cobra, named after a deadly snake. This coaster stood 95 feet high and was 2,210 feet long. Twenty-four riders stood in a train car. An arm strap and a lap bar held the riders in place.

Each year brings new coasters that dive, curve, and drop faster than before. The world's first coaster without a floor opened in 1999. With no tracks above and no floor below, riders really felt the speed of the coaster.

The latest fright is cars that hang down from the tracks. Then they flip the riders over.

People who plan coasters continue to look for new thrills, but roller coasters are not cheap to build. Some of the new ones cost more than eight million dollars. It takes two to three years to plan a new coaster. The planners first build the coaster on a computer.

Next, they have to check for safety. Many of these new rides are hard on the rider's body, so it is important for riders to obey all safety rules on a coaster. As a safe rider, you can enjoy the thrill without any harm. Then you can look for the newest scream machine being built near you!

---

4. What do you think is important to think about if you are going to ride on a scream machine?

Possible Responses

Question 4

You have to make sure it is safe.

This response is based on the text about the safety of roller coasters. Encourage this student to elaborate further. **Ask,** *How would you make sure a roller coaster is safe?*

You have to make sure you are brave enough to ride it. This student connects the idea in the first paragraph. **Ask,** *How would you know if you were brave enough?*

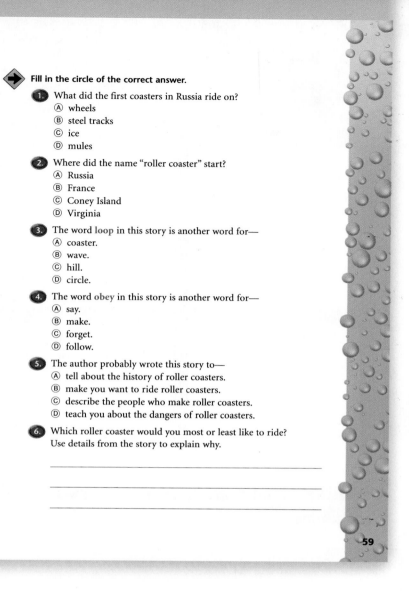

Fill in the circle of the correct answer.

1. What did the first coasters in Russia ride on?
- Ⓐ wheels
- Ⓑ steel tracks
- Ⓒ ice
- Ⓓ mules

2. Where did the name "roller coaster" start?
- Ⓐ Russia
- Ⓑ France
- Ⓒ Coney Island
- Ⓓ Virginia

3. The word **loop** in this story is another word for—
- Ⓐ coaster.
- Ⓑ wave.
- Ⓒ hill.
- Ⓓ circle.

4. The word **obey** in this story is another word for—
- Ⓐ say.
- Ⓑ make.
- Ⓒ forget.
- Ⓓ follow.

5. The author probably wrote this story to—
- Ⓐ tell about the history of roller coasters.
- Ⓑ make you want to ride roller coasters.
- Ⓒ describe the people who make roller coasters.
- Ⓓ teach you about the dangers of roller coasters.

6. Which roller coaster would you most or least like to ride? Use details from the story to explain why.

_____

_____

_____

59

Explain that answering these questions will help students check their comprehension. Answering these questions will also help them practice for other reading tests.

Have students answer the questions. Explain that, as on other tests, each multiple-choice question has one right answer, but the last question can have more than one correct answer.

Answers to Theme Wrap-Up

1. *C. ice* (Literal—Supporting Details)
2. *B. France* (Literal—Supporting Details)
3. *D. circle.* (Inferential—Vocabulary)
4. *D. follow.* (Inferential—Vocabulary)
5. *A. tell about the history of roller coasters.* (Inferential—Main Idea)
6. Accept all reasonable responses, including: *I'd like to go on a Russian ice slide because it traveled at speeds up to 50 miles an hour.* (Inferential—Opinion, Literal—Supporting Details)

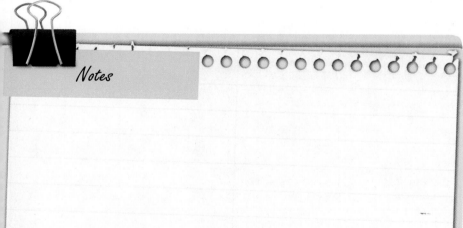

Notes

CHOOSE A CHALLENGE

INTRODUCING THE THEME

Discuss how we all face challenges and that challenges often lead to success.

Explain that something is to be learned or gained from every challenge, and the way to handle challenges is to make good choices.

Model for students how you might fill in one or two boxes in the activity.

Challenges: You could talk about the challenges you face as a teacher or about a challenge you faced when you were your students' age.

Strategies: You could talk about the strategies you use to face challenges now or tell a story about how you dealt with a challenge when you were younger.

Have students work independently to complete the activity. Then have them form pairs to talk about the challenges they and their friends face and how to deal with these challenges. Tell students that the stories they will read in this unit are about challenges—and choices.

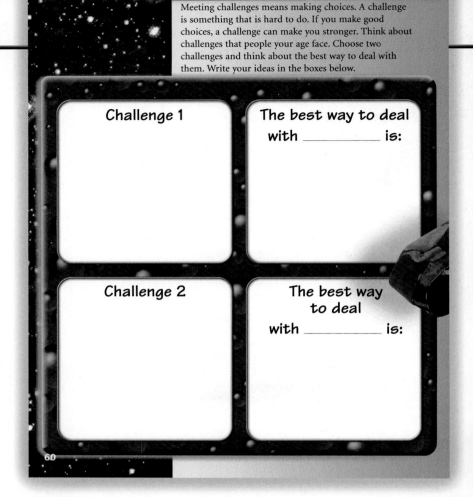

Meeting challenges means making choices. A challenge is something that is hard to do. If you make good choices, a challenge can make you stronger. Think about challenges that people your age face. Choose two challenges and think about the best way to deal with them. Write your ideas in the boxes below.

Challenge 1

The best way to deal with _____ is:

Challenge 2

The best way to deal with _____ is:

60

READING STRATEGIES IN THIS THEME		MAT 8	Stanford 9/10	CTBS/4	Terra Nova
General Reading Strategies	Identifying main idea and details	★	★	★	★
	Identifying facts and opinions	★	★	★	★
Reading Strategies: *Fiction*	Character	★	★	★	★
	Theme	★	★	★	★
Reading Strategies: *Nonfiction*	Interpreting pictures, graphs, and charts	★	★	★	★
	Using research skills and strategies	★	★	★	★

Let's Talk

Think about a challenge you have faced. What choices did you make? What did you learn from the challenge?

61

VOCABULARY IN THIS THEME

Ten vocabulary words are introduced for each selection in this theme. The words are presented first in boldface on the strategy page, then they are the focus of the Vocabulary Builder activity. Further, each word is defined—with pronunciation respelling and the part of speech as it is used in the selection—at the bottom of the page on which it appears. Also, a glossary is provided at the back of the *Workout Book*.

WRITING FORMS IN THIS THEME

Students are guided through structured writing activities that model the writing form and then give students practice writing. Students will learn about the following forms of writing:

- **Instructions**
- **Review**
- **Persuasive Essay**
- **Speech**

ADDITIONAL SKILLS INTRODUCED IN THIS THEME

The *Workout Book* includes activities that help students practice the following skills:

Word Identification Strategies: Phonics
- **Identifying short and long u**
- **Identifying variant consonant g**
- **Identifying variant consonant c**
- **Identifying variant consonant s**

Word Analysis Skills
- **Understanding homonyms, homographs, and homophones**
- **Using prefixes, suffixes, and roots of words**
- **Interpreting figurative language**
- **Using reference materials**

GETTING READY TO READ

STRATEGY FOCUS

Identifying main idea and details

Strategy

IDENTIFYING MAIN IDEA AND DETAILS

Every selection has one main idea and many details that tell the *who, what, when, why, where,* or *how* of the main idea. Understanding the main idea and identifying supporting details are important strategies in comprehending and remembering what has been read.

To determine the main idea of fictional texts, readers must:

- think about the whole story

- summarize the plot and purpose of the story

The activities in this unit will help students apply the strategy of identifying main idea and details.

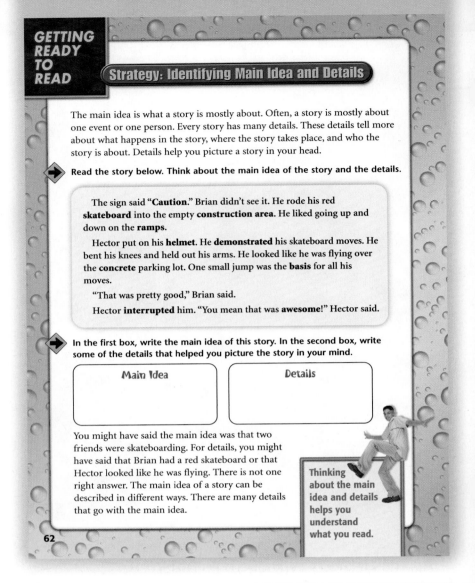

GETTING READY TO READ

Strategy: Identifying Main Idea and Details

The main idea is what a story is mostly about. Often, a story is mostly about one event or one person. Every story has many details. These details tell more about what happens in the story, where the story takes place, and who the story is about. Details help you picture a story in your head.

➤ Read the story below. Think about the main idea of the story and the details.

The sign said "**Caution.**" Brian didn't see it. He rode his red **skateboard** into the empty **construction area.** He liked going up and down on the **ramps.**

Hector put on his **helmet.** He **demonstrated** his skateboard moves. He bent his knees and held out his arms. He looked like he was flying over the **concrete** parking lot. One small jump was the **basis** for all his moves.

"That was pretty good," Brian said.

Hector **interrupted** him. "You mean that was **awesome!**" Hector said.

➤ In the first box, write the main idea of this story. In the second box, write some of the details that helped you picture the story in your mind.

Main Idea	Details

You might have said the main idea was that two friends were skateboarding. For details, you might have said that Brian had a red skateboard or that Hector looked like he was flying. There is not one right answer. The main idea of a story can be described in different ways. There are many details that go with the main idea.

Thinking about the main idea and details helps you understand what you read.

62

INTRODUCING THE STRATEGY

Have students read the story. Then have students fill in the two boxes independently or as a group. Ask students to share their responses in the boxes. Ask questions such as:

- What are some different ways that you described the main idea?

- What are some of the different details you wrote in the second box?

Ask students to share the main idea and some details from some of the other books they are reading or have read. Explain to students that they will use this strategy as they read the selection.

Note: The boldface words on this page are vocabulary words.

The words in the box come from the story you just read. You will see these words again in the story you are about to read.

➡ **Write the correct word in each blank. This will help you think about each word and its meaning. The first one has been done for you.**

skateboard
helmet
interrupted
concrete
basis
demonstrated
caution
construction area
ramps
awesome

1. A board with wheels is called a ___skateboard___.

2. Most _____ sidewalks are good for skating.

3. Letters are the _____ of written words.

4. Before I stopped talking, he _____ me and began talking.

5. To teach him how to throw a ball, she _____ it.

6. The sign on the door of the old house said "_____, keep out!"

7. A place where a building is built is a _____.

8. Instead of using stairs, people in wheelchairs use _____ to go up and down.

9. You could say that something amazing is _____.

10. A _____ keeps your head safe when you skateboard or ride a bike.

Purpose for Reading

Now you are going to read about a boy and girl who skateboard. The place they choose to skateboard might not be safe. Read to find out what happens.

63

Answers to Vocabulary Builder

1. The first answer is provided for students. skateboard
2. concrete
3. basis
4. interrupted
5. demonstrated
6. caution
7. construction area
8. ramps
9. awesome
10. helmet

VOCABULARY EXTENSION

Play a game of vocabulary concentration. Make twenty cards, listing the vocabulary words and their definitions. Lay all of the cards face up for one minute and then turn them face down. Then call on students to match a word and its definition.

Vocabulary Builder

Students are introduced to vocabulary words from the story they will read. Reading the words in context and completing the activity will help build students' confidence prior to reading. For additional reinforcement, the vocabulary words are defined in footnotes throughout the story.

Assessment

To check comprehension of the vocabulary words, arrange students in ten groups and assign each group a word. Have each group write a sentence for the word that shows the meaning of the word. Then, write each sentence on the board with the word missing. Have all students fill in the blanks for all ten sentences.

- awesome
- basis
- caution
- concrete
- construction area
- demonstrated
- helmet
- interrupted
- ramps
- skateboard

Skateboard Sue

SELECTION AT A GLANCE

In this story, a boy named Nick wants to learn skateboarding moves from Skateboard Sue, but he is not sure he wants to break the law to do so.

INTERESTING FACTS

It can look as if skateboarders defy the laws of gravity. The ollie referred to in the story is a small jump that was invented in the late 1970s by a boy named Alan "Ollie" Gelfand. During an ollie, the skateboard appears to stick to the skater's feet in midair. Skateboarders use physics to get the skateboard to stick. Skateboarders get the board to push up by pushing down on the back of the board.

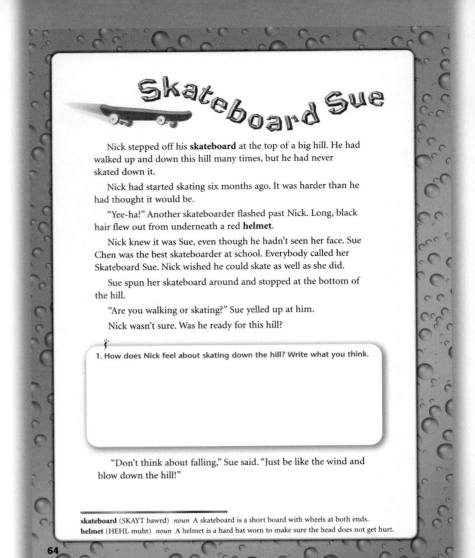

Skateboard Sue

Nick stepped off his **skateboard** at the top of a big hill. He had walked up and down this hill many times, but he had never skated down it.

Nick had started skating six months ago. It was harder than he had thought it would be.

"Yee-ha!" Another skateboarder flashed past Nick. Long, black hair flew out from underneath a red **helmet**.

Nick knew it was Sue, even though he hadn't seen her face. Sue Chen was the best skateboarder at school. Everybody called her Skateboard Sue. Nick wished he could skate as well as she did.

Sue spun her skateboard around and stopped at the bottom of the hill.

"Are you walking or skating?" Sue yelled up at him.

Nick wasn't sure. Was he ready for this hill?

---

1. How does Nick feel about skating down the hill? Write what you think.

"Don't think about falling," Sue said. "Just be like the wind and blow down the hill!"

---

skateboard (SKAYT bawrd) *noun* A skateboard is a short board with wheels at both ends.
helmet (HEHL muht) *noun* A helmet is a hard hat worn to make sure the head does not get hurt.

64

Before Reading

INTRODUCING THE SELECTION

Share with students a time when you wanted to learn something new. Describe how you learned this new activity and who taught you. Ask students to write about a time when they learned something new. What did they learn? What steps did they take to learn it? Who helped them? Tell students the story they will read is about a boy who wants to become a better skateboarder.

During Reading

PURPOSE FOR READING

Students read to find out what happens to Nick.

APPLYING THE STRATEGY

Have students read the story "Skateboard Sue." Explain that they will answer questions while they read the story. Remind them that answering these questions will help them think about the main idea and details in the story.

Possible Responses

Question 1

It is not a big deal.

This student may be writing from personal experience rather than thinking about how Nick feels about the hill. **Say,** *You might think it is not a big deal, but how do you think Nick feels?*

He's nervous.

Encourage this student to link this response to the text. **Say,** *What in the story makes you think that?*

Nick took a deep breath. He stepped on his skateboard and pushed off. A moment later he was flying down the hill. He didn't try to stop at the bottom the way Sue did. Instead, he dragged one foot on the ground to slow himself down. The ride was over too soon. Nick thought about walking back up the hill and doing it again.

"Not bad." Sue's voice **interrupted** his thoughts.

"Thanks," Nick said.

"You should bend your knees a little more," she added.

Nick was glad that his friends weren't watching. They would have made fun of him. Nick was thrilled about skating down that hill without falling. He didn't even mind that Sue was telling him how to skate.

"Next time try to grind the curb on your way down," Sue said.

"I don't know how," Nick said.

interrupted (ihn tuh RUHPT ehd) *verb* To have interrupted someone means to have spoken while he or she was doing something else.

Notes

As students read, tell them that one important idea in the story is that Sue is ready to take risks more quickly than Nick is. Have students take notes of details in the story that describe Sue's and Nick's personalities.

FICTION READING STRATEGY

Character

Explain that characters are the people in a story. We learn about characters from what they do, say, and think.

In this story, the main characters are Nick and Sue. What do readers learn about Nick and Sue? Have students draw the outlines of two heads on a piece of paper and label one "Nick" and one "Sue." Then have students write words that describe each character.

Choose other stories that your students know and ask students to describe the characters in those stories.

"You jump up onto the curb so the **concrete** edge is between the wheels, on this part of the board." Sue pointed to the parts that held the wheels to the skateboard. "Those are called the trucks," she explained. "A grind is when one or both of the trucks scrape against the curb or against whatever you're skating on."

2. Why do you think this move is called a grind?

"I don't think I could do that," Nick said.

"I could show you how," Sue said.

Nick thought Sue was just being polite. Why would she want to skate with him? "No, that's okay. You don't have to do that," he said.

"It's no problem," Sue continued. "Let's meet on Sunday. How about noon at the 14th Street parking lot? Don't be late. I won't wait."

"Well, okay, if you're sure," Nick said. "I guess I could. . . ." Sue was already skating away.

Nick was at the parking lot five minutes early on Sunday. The lot was empty. It was the perfect place to practice.

---

concrete (KAHN kreet) *adjective* Something that is concrete is made of a hard mix of sand, clay, and water.

66

Possible Responses

Question 2

Grinding is like scraping.

This student connects background knowledge of vocabulary and applies it to this story to answer the question.

I'm not sure.

This student may not understand what the word *grind* means. **Say,** *Looking up the word* grind *in the dictionary or asking a friend for the definition will help you answer this question.*

As he waited for Sue, Nick did an "ollie." This jump was the **basis** of most skateboard tricks. He stood on the board with one foot toward the front and the other foot near the tail. Nick pushed down hard, smacking the tail of the board against the ground. This made the front of the board pop up into the air.

> 3. Why do you think skaters should learn to do an ollie before they learn other tricks?

"Ready to do some curb grinds?" Sue asked as she skated up to him.

There was a curb along the side of the parking lot. Sue **demonstrated** the trick for Nick. Then, Nick tried it. The front of his skateboard hit the concrete.

---

basis (BAY sihs) *noun* A basis means a beginning point.
demonstrated (DEHM uhn strayt ehd) *verb* To have demonstrated something means to have shown someone how to do it.

67

Encourage students from other countries to share with the class their experiences with skateboarding. **Ask,** *Is skateboarding American or do people skateboard in other countries? What other sports or activities are popular with young people in other countries?*

RECIPROCAL TEACHING

Summarize

Have students summarize the story. Start by having them write the main idea of the story in one or two sentences at the top of a page. Then have them list the details from the story that tell *who, what, when, where, why,* and *how.*

Question 3

It's easy. I know how to do one.

This student makes a personal connection with the story.

Because it's just a little jump.

This student uses the text details to provide an accurate description of what an ollie might look like and to conclude that it is a basic trick. **Ask,** *Why do you think skaters should learn it first?*

After Reading

It is very important to have students read and discuss the story and their responses to the questions in the boxes.

DISCUSSING THE RESPONSES

- Call on different volunteers to share their responses to the questions in the boxes.
- Ask students to explain what in their experiences or in the story made them answer each question as they did.
- Ask students how answering the questions in the boxes helped them think about what they read.

RETEACHING

If students are having trouble responding to the questions in the boxes, **say,** *The questions are there to help you think about what you are reading. Don't worry about whether your answer is right or wrong. If you are having trouble answering the questions, re-read the paragraph before the question and then write whatever the question makes you think.*

Model for students the process you use in answering one of the questions. **Say,** *When I answered the first question, I thought Nick was nervous because he had not gone down the hill before but he was also excited to try because he just saw Sue skate it.*

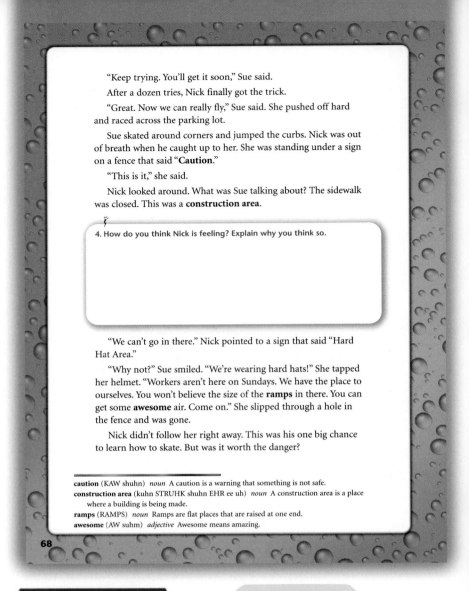

"Keep trying. You'll get it soon," Sue said.

After a dozen tries, Nick finally got the trick.

"Great. Now we can really fly," Sue said. She pushed off hard and raced across the parking lot.

Sue skated around corners and jumped the curbs. Nick was out of breath when he caught up to her. She was standing under a sign on a fence that said "**Caution**."

"This is it," she said.

Nick looked around. What was Sue talking about? The sidewalk was closed. This was a **construction area**.

> 4. How do you think Nick is feeling? Explain why you think so.

"We can't go in there." Nick pointed to a sign that said "Hard Hat Area."

"Why not?" Sue smiled. "We're wearing hard hats!" She tapped her helmet. "Workers aren't here on Sundays. We have the place to ourselves. You won't believe the size of the **ramps** in there. You can get some **awesome** air. Come on." She slipped through a hole in the fence and was gone.

Nick didn't follow her right away. This was his one big chance to learn how to skate. But was it worth the danger?

caution (KAW shuhn) *noun* A caution is a warning that something is not safe.
construction area (kuhn STRUHK shuhn EHR ee uh) *noun* A construction area is a place where a building is being made.
ramps (RAMPS) *noun* Ramps are flat places that are raised at one end.
awesome (AW suhm) *adjective* Awesome means amazing.

68

Assessment

Informal Assessment
To assess students' understanding, use their written responses in the boxes and their oral explanations for what they wrote.

Student Self-Assessment
Encourage students to think about their own reading experience by having them respond to this question: *How does answering questions while you read help you think about what you are reading?*

Possible Responses

Question 4

Excited

Encourage the student to make the connection between this response and the text. **Say,** *What in the story makes you think he is excited?*

He's nervous because he doesn't think they should go in there.

This response gives an accurate description of Nick's feelings based on text details. Encourage such responses.

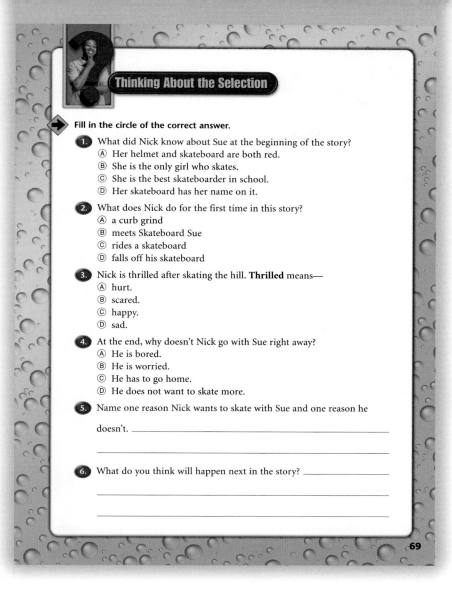

Fill in the circle of the correct answer.

1. What did Nick know about Sue at the beginning of the story?
   Ⓐ Her helmet and skateboard are both red.
   Ⓑ She is the only girl who skates.
   Ⓒ She is the best skateboarder in school.
   Ⓓ Her skateboard has her name on it.

2. What does Nick do for the first time in this story?
   Ⓐ a curb grind
   Ⓑ meets Skateboard Sue
   Ⓒ rides a skateboard
   Ⓓ falls off his skateboard

3. Nick is thrilled after skating the hill. **Thrilled** means—
   Ⓐ hurt.
   Ⓑ scared.
   Ⓒ happy.
   Ⓓ sad.

4. At the end, why doesn't Nick go with Sue right away?
   Ⓐ He is bored.
   Ⓑ He is worried.
   Ⓒ He has to go home.
   Ⓓ He does not want to skate more.

5. Name one reason Nick wants to skate with Sue and one reason he

   doesn't. _____
   _____

6. What do you think will happen next in the story? _____
   _____
   _____

69

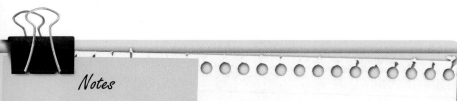

Notes

Thinking About the Selection

Explain that answering these questions will help students check their comprehension of the story. Answering these questions will also help them practice for other reading tests.

Have students answer the questions. Explain that, as on other tests, each multiple-choice question has one right answer, but the last two questions can be answered in different ways.

Answers to Thinking About the Selection

1. **C. She is the best skateboarder in school.** (Literal—Supporting Details/Character)
2. **A. a curb grind** (Literal—Sequence/Plot)
3. **C. happy.** (Inferential—Vocabulary/Character)
4. **B. He is worried.** (Inferential—Cause-Effect/Character)
5. Accept all reasonable responses, including: *He wants to learn more, but he doesn't want to get into trouble.* (Inferential—Main Idea/Plot)
6. Accept all reasonable responses, including: *Nick will follow Sue, but they will get into trouble.* (Inferential—Making Predictions/Plot)

Students who enjoyed "Skateboard Sue" might want to read the entire book, *Skateboard City.* Students might also enjoy reading other books about learning how to do things.

Reading Aloud

- *The Apprentice* by Pilar Llorente (Farrar, Straus & Giroux, Inc., 1994). [F]
- *Basketball the Right Way* by Robin Roberts (Millbrook, 2000). [NF]
- *Incredible Everything* by Richard Platt & Stephen Biesty (DK Publishing, 1997). [NF]
- *Josefina Learns a Lesson* by Valerie Tripp (Pleasant Company, 1997). [F]
- *Learn to Draw 3-D* by Doug Dubosque (Peel Productions, 1992). [NF]

Independent Reading

- *It Goes Eeeeeeeee!* by Jamie Gilson (Houghton Mifflin, 2001). [F]

FAMILY INVOLVEMENT

Have students talk with family members, both younger and older, about activities and skills they have taught each other to do. Have each student make a list. As a class, compile a list of things learned and of things taught and the role students played in each.

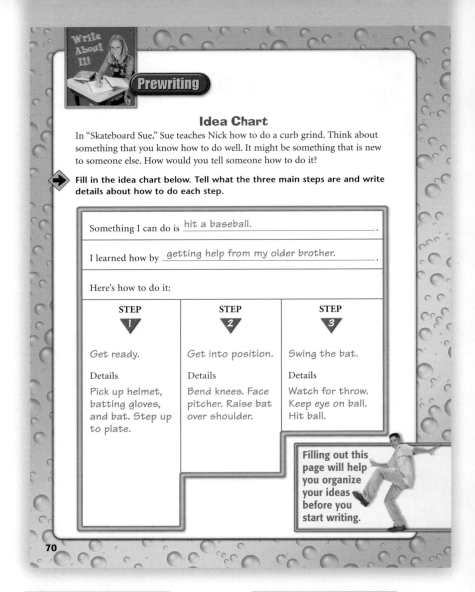

Write About It!

Prewriting

Idea Chart

In "Skateboard Sue," Sue teaches Nick how to do a curb grind. Think about something that you know how to do well. It might be something that is new to someone else. How would you tell someone how to do it?

➡ **Fill in the idea chart below. Tell what the three main steps are and write details about how to do each step.**

Something I can do is _hit a baseball._

I learned how by _getting help from my older brother._

Here's how to do it:

STEP 1	STEP 2	STEP 3
Get ready.	Get into position.	Swing the bat.
Details	Details	Details
Pick up helmet, batting gloves, and bat. Step up to plate.	Bend knees. Face pitcher. Raise bat over shoulder.	Watch for throw. Keep eye on ball. Hit ball.

Filling out this page will help you organize your ideas before you start writing.

70

Before Writing

Have students brainstorm things they can do well and make lists on paper. If students are having trouble generating ideas, talk to them about their interests. **Say,** *What do you enjoy doing?* It is likely that students have some expertise in the activities they enjoy.

Or, have students work in small groups to brainstorm ideas before they begin working independently on their charts.

During Writing

Have students refer to their charts. Personalize the experience for students having difficulty. **Say,** *What is something that you do often? How would you tell somebody else how to do that?*

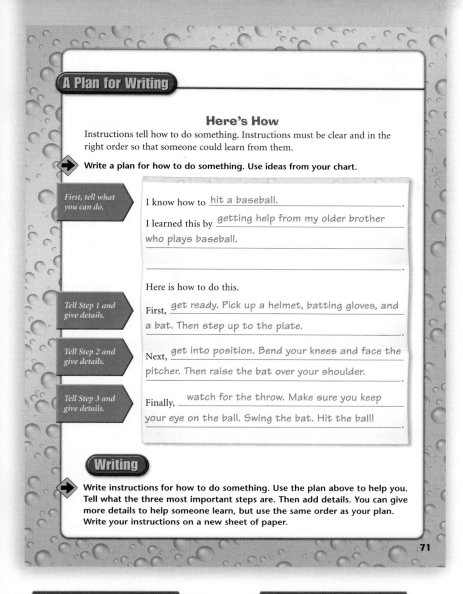

A Plan for Writing

Here's How

Instructions tell how to do something. Instructions must be clear and in the right order so that someone could learn from them.

➤ **Write a plan for how to do something. Use ideas from your chart.**

First, tell what you can do.

I know how to ___hit a baseball.___

I learned this by ___getting help from my older brother who plays baseball.___

Tell Step 1 and give details.

Here is how to do this.

First, ___get ready. Pick up a helmet, batting gloves, and a bat. Then step up to the plate.___

Tell Step 2 and give details.

Next, ___get into position. Bend your knees and face the pitcher. Then raise the bat over your shoulder.___

Tell Step 3 and give details.

Finally, ___watch for the throw. Make sure you keep your eye on the ball. Swing the bat. Hit the ball!___

Writing

➤ Write instructions for how to do something. Use the plan above to help you. Tell what the three most important steps are. Then add details. You can give more details to help someone learn, but use the same order as your plan. Write your instructions on a new sheet of paper.

71

After Writing

As a group, discuss students' reactions to what they have written. On the board, make a list of the many different skills and talents the students have.

GROUP SHARING

Pair students to share instructions. Have one partner play the learner, giving the writer feedback on how clear the instructions are. Then have partners switch roles. Have a pair demonstrate how to follow one partner's instructions.

Assessment

Portfolio Assessment
Students may want to save their instructions in their classroom portfolios.

Student Self-Assessment
Encourage students to think about their writing experience. **Say,** *What did instructing someone in doing something make you realize about your own strengths? Why is it important to share your skills with others?*

71

Breaking the Code

Short u

Ask a volunteer to read aloud the rule about **short u.** Point out that each example of a **short u** word (*bus, sun,* and *rug*) has only one vowel.

Read the directions for the activity aloud. Discuss the first sentence. If students are having difficulty, read the sentence and answer choices aloud, exaggerating the **short u** sound. Remind students that the answer should have the same *u* sound as *bus, sun,* or *rug.* Have students complete the second sentence independently.

Long u

Ask a volunteer to read aloud the rule about **long u.** Point out that each of the **long u** examples (*blue, mule,* and *flute*) ends with a silent *e.*

Read the directions for the activity aloud. Discuss the third sentence. If students are having difficulty, read the sentence and answer choices aloud, exaggerating the **long u** sound. Remind students that the answer should have the same *u* sound as *blue, mule,* or *flute.* Have students complete the fourth sentence independently.

Have students complete sentences five through eight independently.

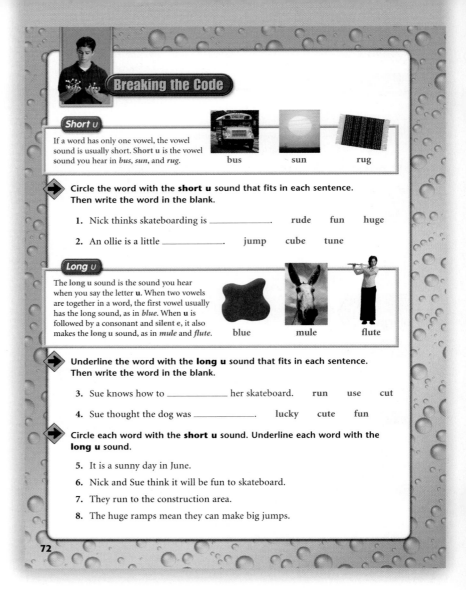

Breaking the Code

Short u

If a word has only one vowel, the vowel sound is usually short. Short u is the vowel sound you hear in *bus, sun,* and *rug.*

bus   sun   rug

➤ Circle the word with the **short u** sound that fits in each sentence. Then write the word in the blank.

1. Nick thinks skateboarding is _____.   rude   fun   huge

2. An ollie is a little _____.   jump   cube   tune

Long u

The long u sound is the sound you hear when you say the letter **u.** When two vowels are together in a word, the first vowel usually has the long sound, as in *blue.* When **u** is followed by a consonant and silent e, it also makes the long u sound, as in *mule* and *flute.*

blue   mule   flute

➤ Underline the word with the **long u** sound that fits in each sentence. Then write the word in the blank.

3. Sue knows how to _____ her skateboard.   run   use   cut

4. Sue thought the dog was _____.   lucky   cute   fun

➤ Circle each word with the **short u** sound. Underline each word with the **long u** sound.

5. It is a sunny day in June.
6. Nick and Sue think it will be fun to skateboard.
7. They run to the construction area.
8. The huge ramps mean they can make big jumps.

72

Answers to Breaking the Code

1. (fun)
2. (jump)
3. <u>use</u>
4. <u>cute</u>
5. (sunny) <u>June</u>
6. <u>Sue</u> (fun)
7. (run) (construction)
8. <u>huge</u> (jumps)

RETEACHING

Pair students and have them play a game of tick-tack-toe using words instead of *X*'s and *O*'s. Have one student use only words with a **short u** sound. Have the other use words with the **long u** sound. Then they should take turns, each trying to get three in a row. If students need help coming up with **short u** or **long u** words, write a list on the board: *use, cute, June, cube, tune, tube, rule, huge, jug, tub, bus, bug, hug, mud, tug, sun, fun, jump.*

72

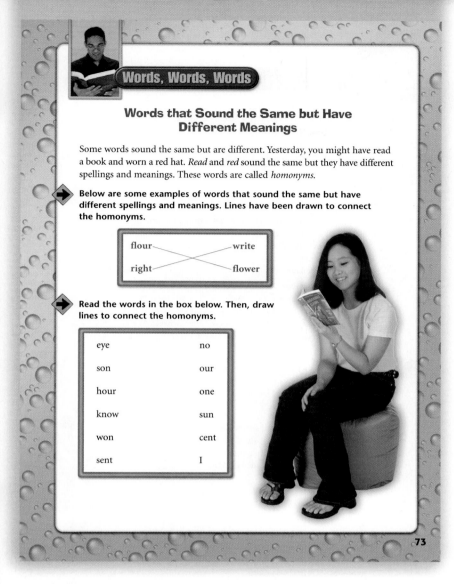

Words, Words, Words

Words that Sound the Same but Have Different Meanings

Some words sound the same but are different. Yesterday, you might have read a book and worn a red hat. *Read* and *red* sound the same but they have different spellings and meanings. These words are called *homonyms*.

➤ Below are some examples of words that sound the same but have different spellings and meanings. Lines have been drawn to connect the homonyms.

flour	write
right	flower

➤ Read the words in the box below. Then, draw lines to connect the homonyms.

eye	no
son	our
hour	one
know	sun
won	cent
sent	I

73

Words, Words, Words

Explain that some words sound the same but are spelled differently and have different meanings. The way to tell the meaning of the word is to read or listen to the way the word is used.

Write the following sentences on the board and have a volunteer read them aloud:

Jim picked a <u>flower</u> for Maria.

Jim added some <u>flour</u> to the cookie dough.

Then **ask,** *Could someone tell me the difference between* flower *and* flour? Elicit from students that a flower is part of a plant and flour is used in cooking. Ask which words from the sentences helped students know which kind of *flour* was intended.

Have students complete the activity titled Words that Sound the Same but Have Different Meanings.

RETEACHING

Make a list of homonyms: *guessed/guest, past/passed, aloud/allowed, sent/cent, some/sum,* and *mail/male.* Divide the class into two teams. Have each team choose a volunteer to go to the board and write two sentences using a pair of homonyms. Give each team two help cards that can be used to get help from the team if needed. Each sentence in which the word is used correctly earns a point. Continue until each team has written sentences for three pairs of homonyms.

Answers to Words, Words, Words

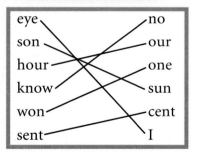

eye	no
son	our
hour	one
know	sun
won	cent
sent	I

REINFORCING THE THEME

To reinforce the theme *Choose a Challenge,* have students think about a new activity they started. How did their lives change after they began the new activity? On paper have students write "Life Before _____" on the left side and "Life After _____" on the right side, then list ways their life changed. Tell students they will read about how skateboarding has changed over the years.

STRATEGY FOCUS

Identifying main idea and details

Strategy

IDENTIFYING MAIN IDEA AND DETAILS

Understanding and distinguishing between main idea and details are crucial to comprehending informational text. In these texts, the title and the first and last paragraphs usually state the main idea. Other paragraphs usually focus on details to support the main idea.

Readers should:

- read and think about the title and the main idea of the first and last paragraphs, and

- read and think about the details in the text body.

The activities in this unit will help students apply the strategy of identifying main idea and details.

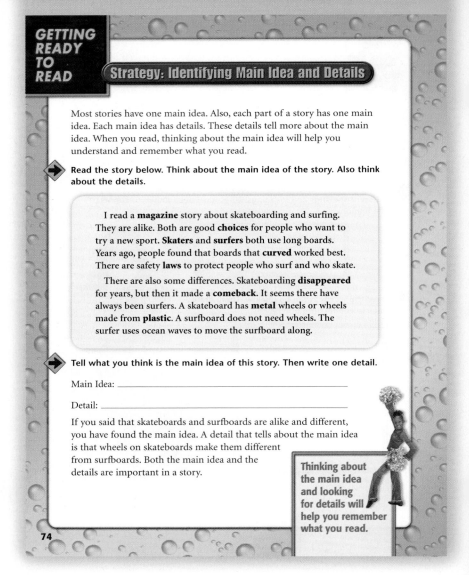

Strategy: Identifying Main Idea and Details

Most stories have one main idea. Also, each part of a story has one main idea. Each main idea has details. These details tell more about the main idea. When you read, thinking about the main idea will help you understand and remember what you read.

➡ **Read the story below. Think about the main idea of the story. Also think about the details.**

I read a **magazine** story about skateboarding and surfing. They are alike. Both are good **choices** for people who want to try a new sport. **Skaters** and **surfers** both use long boards. Years ago, people found that boards that **curved** worked best. There are safety **laws** to protect people who surf and who skate.

There are also some differences. Skateboarding **disappeared** for years, but then it made a **comeback**. It seems there have always been surfers. A skateboard has **metal** wheels or wheels made from **plastic**. A surfboard does not need wheels. The surfer uses ocean waves to move the surfboard along.

➡ **Tell what you think is the main idea of this story. Then write one detail.**

Main Idea: _____

Detail: _____

If you said that skateboards and surfboards are alike and different, you have found the main idea. A detail that tells about the main idea is that wheels on skateboards make them different from surfboards. Both the main idea and the details are important in a story.

Thinking about the main idea and looking for details will help you remember what you read.

74

INTRODUCING THE STRATEGY

Have students read the selection. Then, independently or in groups, have students write the main idea and one detail. Ask questions such as:

- Which sentences in the paragraphs stated the main idea?

- Which sentences told details?

Explain that the exact words students used to write the main idea and the details they selected are not the most important thing. It is more important that they can identify and distinguish the difference between the main idea and details. Explain to students that they will use this strategy as they read the selection, "The Story of Skateboarding."

Note: The boldface words on this page are vocabulary words.

The words in the box come from the story you just read. You will see these words again in the story you are about to read.

disappeared
skaters
metal
choices
plastic,
surfers
magazine
curved
comeback
laws

Complete the crossword puzzle. This will help you think about each word and its meaning. The first word has been done for you.

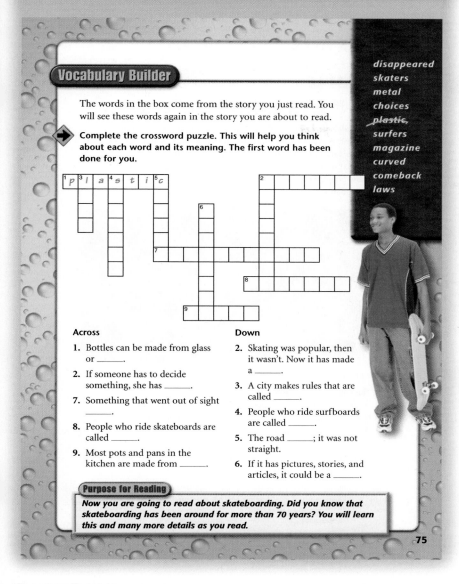

Across

1. Bottles can be made from glass or _____.
2. If someone has to decide something, she has _____.
7. Something that went out of sight _____.
8. People who ride skateboards are called _____.
9. Most pots and pans in the kitchen are made from _____.

Down

2. Skating was popular, then it wasn't. Now it has made a _____.
3. A city makes rules that are called _____.
4. People who ride surfboards are called _____.
5. The road _____; it was not straight.
6. If it has pictures, stories, and articles, it could be a _____.

Purpose for Reading

Now you are going to read about skateboarding. Did you know that skateboarding has been around for more than 70 years? You will learn this and many more details as you read.

75

Vocabulary Builder

Students are introduced to vocabulary words from the selection they will read. Reading the words in context and completing the activity will help students understand the words when they encounter them in the reading selection. For additional reinforcement, the vocabulary words are defined in footnotes throughout the story.

Assessment

Check students' comprehension by having them write synonyms, antonyms, or related words for each of the ten vocabulary words.

- **choices**
- **comeback**
- **curved**
- **disappeared**
- **laws**
- **magazine**
- **metal**
- **plastic**
- **skaters**
- **surfers**

Answers to Vocabulary Builder

Across

1. **plastic**
2. **choices**
7. **disappeared**
8. **skaters**
9. **metal**

Down

2. **comeback**
3. **laws**
4. **surfers**
5. **curved**
6. **magazine**

VOCABULARY EXTENSION

Divide the class into two teams. Give each team five of the vocabulary words. Have each team tell the other team clues for each word without using the word itself. If the other team can guess with just one clue, give three points; with two clues, give two points; with three clues, give one point. Reward the winning team with a small prize.

The Story of Skateboarding

SELECTION AT A GLANCE

SELECTION AT A GLANCE

This selection tells the history of the sport of skateboarding.

INTERESTING FACTS

Although skateboarders do not compete at the Olympic Games, they have their own competition: the X Games.

The X Games were first held in 1995 and included sports like bungee jumping, windsurfing, and mountain biking. Today, competitors from around the world compete annually in both the X Games and the Winter X Games.

The Story of Skateboarding

Skateboarding has had a bumpy ride for more than 70 years. Sometimes it has been more popular than at other times, but skateboarding has never **disappeared**. Now, skateboarding is popular again. It seems that it may be here to stay. What makes so many people love this sport? To find out, check out the story of skateboarding.

Skaters in the 1960s didn't wear gear.

The Ride Begins

Skateboards were first used in the 1930s. **Skaters** joined boards to **metal** roller-skate wheels. The hard metal wheels of the skateboards would bang along sidewalks.

Kids couldn't get better wheels. They didn't have other **choices**. Stores didn't sell skateboards until about 25 years after the skateboard was invented.

---

disappeared (dihs uh PIHRD) *verb* Disappeared means went out of sight.
skaters (SKAYT uhrz) *noun* Skaters are people who ride skateboards.
metal (MEHT l) *adjective* Metal means made of iron or another shiny solid, such as silver.
choices (CHOYS uhz) *noun* Choices are things that you choose between.

76

Before Reading

INTRODUCING THE SELECTION

Ask a volunteer to read the first line of the selection: "Skateboarding has had a bumpy ride for more than 70 years." Explain that the first sentence gives clues about the main idea of this passage. Then ask students to write several sentences about what details of information they think will be included in the rest of the selection. Have students share their ideas before they begin reading.

During Reading

PURPOSE FOR READING

Students read to learn about the history of skateboarding.

APPLYING THE STRATEGY

Have students read the selection "The Story of Skateboarding." Explain that they will answer Think-Along questions while they read the selection. Remind them that answering these questions will help them think about the main idea and details of the selection.

Notes

Skateboards at the Store

In 1958, toy makers began to design and make skateboards. The first skateboards sold in stores were made of wood. A few were made from **plastic**. Wooden boards were heavy and didn't bend very much. Plastic boards bent too much.

Soon toy makers began using clay wheels on skateboards. Clay wheels didn't make as much noise as metal wheels.

1. What do you think about these early skateboards?

Skating Becomes Popular

In the early 1960s, skateboarding became very popular. **Surfers** were interested in skateboarding. Surfers rode waves like skaters rode on land. They listened to songs such as "Surfin' U.S.A." by the Beach Boys. There was one problem. Surfers could only surf at the beach during good weather.

Surfers began skating. They called it sidewalk surfing. A new song came out by Jan and Dean called "Sidewalk Surfing." Thanks to the surfers, skating was bigger than ever.

plastic (PLAS tihk) *noun* Plastic is a solid used to make strong objects.
surfers (SURF uhrz) *noun* Surfers are people who ride ocean waves on surfboards.

77

Question 1

They don't seem that fun to ride.

This response shows the student has thought about and made a personal connection with the details so far.

I don't know.

Encourage this student to respond to the question. Say, *What do you think it would have been like to ride the early skateboards?*

Strategy Tip

After reading, divide students into five groups. Assign each group a time period from the selection: 1930–1960, 1960–1970, 1970–1980, 1980–1990, and 1990–today. Have each group write a brief summary of the details provided about skateboarding during each time period.

NONFICTION READING STRATEGY

Pictures, Graphs, and Charts

Have students graph the rise and fall of the popularity of skateboarding, starting with 1930 and ending with today. Have them draw 10-year increments on the y-axis and "Very Popular," "Somewhat Popular," and "Not Popular" on the x-axis. Then have them plot the degree of popularity. Students' graphs might look something like this.

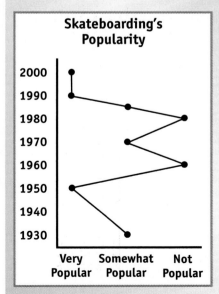

Skateboarding's Popularity

MEETING
INDIVIDUAL
NEEDS

If students are having difficulty answering the questions in the boxes, remind them that there are no right or wrong answers to the Think-Along questions. **Say,** *The questions are there to help you think about what you read. There are no right or wrong answers. Just write what you think in response to each question.*

Skating Comes and Goes

In 1965, everyone saw the first National Skateboard Championship on TV. A **magazine** ran a story on the thrills and dangers of skating. Doctors also pointed out the dangers of skating. Suddenly everyone was talking about skateboarding. By the end of 1965, skating didn't seem so cool anymore. Many skaters stopped skating.

> 2. Do you think early skateboarding was safe? Explain why you do or don't think so.

In 1971, Richard Stevenson designed a board that **curved** up at the back. This tail made the board easier to move. In 1973, surfer Frank Nasworthy found a better wheel for skateboards. The wheel was made of a new kind of plastic. The wheel was strong, but softer than clay. Frank tried out the new wheels. They made his ride smoother and quieter. The wheels were named Cadillacs because they rode as smoothly as Cadillac cars.

In a few years, skating had made another **comeback**. Kids skated in empty swimming pools and city streets. Skaters also rode in new skate parks. Some kids still rode on wooden boards. Others used new boards that were made from wood and plastic. These boards were strong and could slide really well.

magazine (MAG uh zeen) *noun* A magazine is a paper booklet that has stories and pictures in it.
curved (KURVD) *verb* Curved means rounded or bent like part of a circle.
comeback (KUHM bak) *noun* A comeback happens when a person or thing that used to be popular becomes popular again.

78

Possible Responses

Question 2

I guess it wasn't safe just because it says doctors warned about it.

This student draws upon one detail from the selection. Encourage the student to connect this with other details. **Say,** *What did you read in the story that might tell you why doctors thought this was not safe?*

It couldn't be dangerous because you couldn't go fast.

This response does not take into account some of the story details. **Say,** *Does the paragraph say that some people thought it was dangerous?*

78

More Ups and Downs

In the early 1980s, skating was on its way out again. City governments had passed skating **laws**. These laws said that skaters couldn't skate on sidewalks or streets. The country of Norway didn't let anyone skate at all! The laws were passed because people were worried that skaters could get hurt.

Skating wasn't gone for very long. In the late 1980s, it was back again. Skateboarders built ramps and skated in their backyards. New skateboards had curved ends that made the boards stronger and easier to move.

Skaters started dressing in a certain way. They wore big T-shirts and long shorts. Lots of kids listened to music while they skated. For many, skating had become a way of life.

> 3. Why do you think skateboarding became so popular?

laws (LAWZ) *noun* Laws are rules made by a city, state, or country. Laws tell you what you can and cannot do.

79

Students not originally from the United States may benefit from a brief discussion of American cultural history to put this selection into context. What was happening in the United States in the 1930s, 1940s, 1950s, 1960s, 1970s, 1980s, and 1990s? Discuss and have the class generate a list of key events or words to describe each decade.

RECIPROCAL TEACHING

Question

Have each student generate one question that can be answered by the text. Compile all of the questions and administer them as a comprehension assessment. After students answer all questions, have them discuss their responses and identify the section of text that had the answer to each question.

Question 3

It was cool.

This response shows that the student is thinking about the selection and the question. In discussion, encourage further elaboration. **Say,** *What made it cool?*

The changes

This student may be thinking about the selection, but that is not clear from this response. Encourage further elaboration. **Say,** *There were a lot of changes. Which ones do you think made skating popular?*

After Reading

Have different students share their responses aloud to emphasize the many possible responses to the Think-Along questions in the boxes.

DISCUSSING THE RESPONSES

• Pair students and have them share and discuss their responses.

• Have students write about how their responses were different from their partner's.

• Ask students how answering the Think-Along questions and discussing them with a partner helped them think about what they read.

RETEACHING

For those students who are having difficulty, complete this activity as a group.

Write the main idea of the selection on the board: *Skateboarding has had a bumpy ride.* Then, draw a two-column table. On the left, write *Highs*. On the right, write *Lows*. Have students re-read the selection and identify the high and low points in the history of skateboarding. Write a brief note about each one in the table.

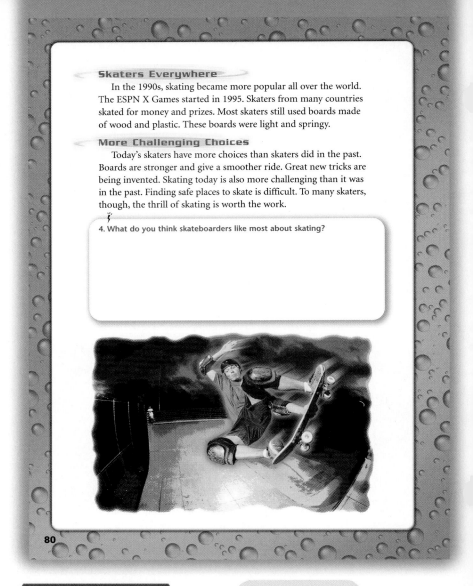

Skaters Everywhere

In the 1990s, skating became more popular all over the world. The ESPN X Games started in 1995. Skaters from many countries skated for money and prizes. Most skaters still used boards made of wood and plastic. These boards were light and springy.

More Challenging Choices

Today's skaters have more choices than skaters did in the past. Boards are stronger and give a smoother ride. Great new tricks are being invented. Skating today is also more challenging than it was in the past. Finding safe places to skate is difficult. To many skaters, though, the thrill of skating is worth the work.

4. What do you think skateboarders like most about skating?

80

Assessment

Informal Assessment
To assess students' understanding, use their written responses in the boxes and their oral explanations for what they wrote.

Student Self-Assessment
Encourage students to think about their own reading experience by having them respond to this question: *How well did you understand this selection?*

Possible Responses

Question 4

They like being different.

This response demonstrates comprehension of the selection and perhaps the application of background knowledge.

The tricks

This response is supported by the information in the selection and demonstrates that the student is connecting with the text.

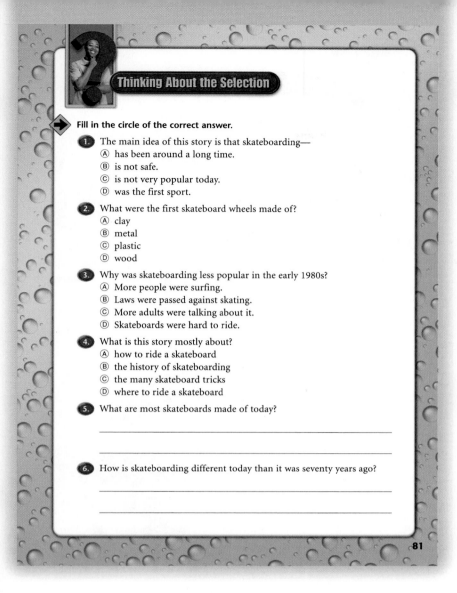

Thinking About the Selection

Fill in the circle of the correct answer.

1. The main idea of this story is that skateboarding—
   Ⓐ has been around a long time.
   Ⓑ is not safe.
   Ⓒ is not very popular today.
   Ⓓ was the first sport.

2. What were the first skateboard wheels made of?
   Ⓐ clay
   Ⓑ metal
   Ⓒ plastic
   Ⓓ wood

3. Why was skateboarding less popular in the early 1980s?
   Ⓐ More people were surfing.
   Ⓑ Laws were passed against skating.
   Ⓒ More adults were talking about it.
   Ⓓ Skateboards were hard to ride.

4. What is this story mostly about?
   Ⓐ how to ride a skateboard
   Ⓑ the history of skateboarding
   Ⓒ the many skateboard tricks
   Ⓓ where to ride a skateboard

5. What are most skateboards made of today?

   _____
   _____

6. How is skateboarding different today than it was seventy years ago?

   _____
   _____

81

Thinking About the Selection

Explain that answering these questions will help students check their comprehension. Answering these questions will also help them practice for other reading tests.

Have students answer the questions. Explain that, as on other tests, each multiple-choice question has one right answer, but the last two questions can be answered in different ways.

Answers to
Thinking About the Selection

1. ***A. has been around a long time.*** (Inferential—Main Idea)

2. ***B. metal*** (Literal— Supporting Details)

3. ***B. Laws were passed against skating.*** (Inferential—Cause-Effect)

4. ***B. the history of skateboarding*** (Inferential—Main Idea)

5. Accept all reasonable responses, including: *Wood and plastic* (Literal—Supporting Details)

6. Accept all reasonable responses, including: *It is a smoother ride and it is more popular.* (Literal—Supporting Details)

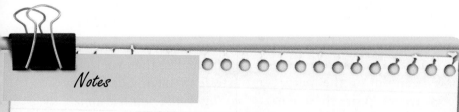

Notes

Students who enjoyed "The Story of Skateboarding" might want to read the entire book, *The Thrill of the Ride*. Students also might enjoy reading other books about skateboarding and similar sports.

Reading Aloud

- *Inline Skater* by Matt Christopher (Little Brown, 2001). [F]
- *In-Line Skating* by Aldie Chalmers (Millbrook, 1997). [NF]
- *Mountain Biking* by Brant Richards (Millbrook, 1998). [NF]
- *Skateboard Tough* by Matt Christopher (Little, Brown, 1994). [F]
- *Snowboarding* by Leslie McKenna (Millbrook, 1998). [NF]

Independent Reading

- *Knight Moves* by Pam Cardiff (Steck-Vaughn, 1995). [F]

FAMILY INVOLVEMENT

Have each student talk to an adult family member about a product that young people enjoyed which was popular when the adult was younger. Have students ask the adult what other people thought about this product. If possible, have students bring in the object from home. Volunteers can then share these stories and objects with classmates.

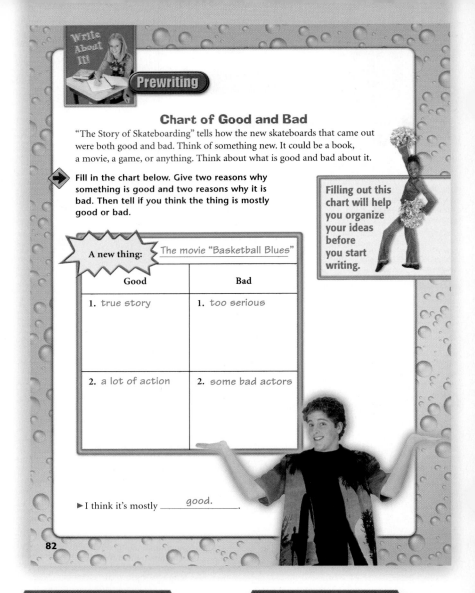

Prewriting

Chart of Good and Bad

"The Story of Skateboarding" tells how the new skateboards that came out were both good and bad. Think of something new. It could be a book, a movie, a game, or anything. Think about what is good and bad about it.

Fill in the chart below. Give two reasons why something is good and two reasons why it is bad. Then tell if you think the thing is mostly good or bad.

Filling out this chart will help you organize your ideas before you start writing.

A new thing: The movie "Basketball Blues"

Good	Bad
1. true story	1. too serious
2. a lot of action	2. some bad actors

▶ I think it's mostly _____good._____ .

82

Before Writing

Have students brainstorm products and creations that have been put on the market in recent years. Write these ideas on the board. If students are having trouble generating ideas, talk to them about the things they buy or enjoy. Say, *What was something that came out lately that you felt you had to buy or see?*

Or, have students work in small groups to brainstorm ideas before they begin working independently on their charts.

During Writing

Refer students to their charts. Personalize the experience for students having difficulty. Say, *Why would you tell somebody to buy or see something?*

After Writing

Discuss students' reactions to what they have written. Make a list of the products the class reviewed. Divide the list into things that students would recommend and things they would not.

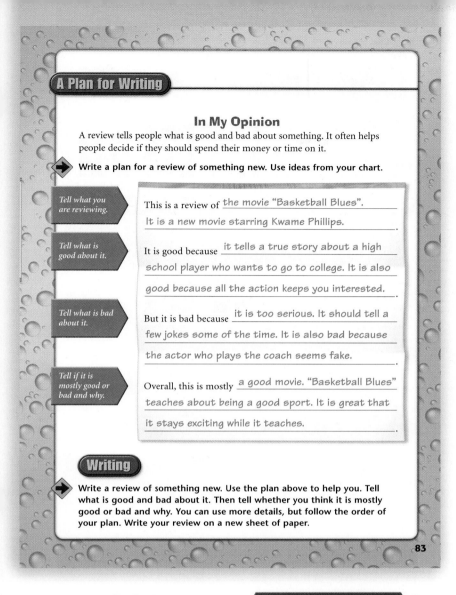

A Plan for Writing

In My Opinion

A review tells people what is good and bad about something. It often helps people decide if they should spend their money or time on it.

➤ Write a plan for a review of something new. Use ideas from your chart.

Tell what you are reviewing.

This is a review of *the movie "Basketball Blues".*
It is a new movie starring Kwame Phillips.

Tell what is good about it.

It is good because *it tells a true story about a high*
school player who wants to go to college. It is also
good because all the action keeps you interested.

Tell what is bad about it.

But it is bad because *it is too serious. It should tell a*
few jokes some of the time. It is also bad because
the actor who plays the coach seems fake.

Tell if it is mostly good or bad and why.

Overall, this is mostly *a good movie. "Basketball Blues"*
teaches about being a good sport. It is great that
it stays exciting while it teaches.

Writing

➤ Write a review of something new. Use the plan above to help you. Tell what is good and bad about it. Then tell whether you think it is mostly good or bad and why. You can use more details, but follow the order of your plan. Write your review on a new sheet of paper.

83

GROUP SHARING

Organize students into groups to compare their completed reviews. Have groups find out if someone in the group has a different opinion on something that was reviewed. Have students with different opinions on product reviews debate their positions in front of the class.

Assessment

Portfolio Assessment
Students may want to save their reviews in their classroom portfolios.

Student Self-Assessment
Encourage students to think about their writing experience. Say, *What did reviewing something make you realize about what you like or dislike? What does it make you realize about what other people like and dislike?*

SCORING RUBRIC: REVIEWS

SCORE 3

Review is convincing and states a clear opinion. Topic is clearly defined and supporting details are well developed. Contains clear, vivid sensory details. Writing is organized and coherent. Contains few errors in sentence structure, usage, mechanics, or spelling.

SCORE 2

Review is convincing and states an opinion. Topic is defined and supporting ideas are developed. Contains sensory details, but some are not vivid; some may not be clear. Has some degree of organization and coherence. Contains some errors in sentence structure, usage, mechanics, or spelling.

SCORE 1

Review is not convincing and may not state an opinion. Topic is not clearly defined or supporting details are weak. Writing contains few or no sensory details and most are not vivid or clear. Has minimal organization and coherence. Contains many errors in sentence structure, usage, mechanics, or spelling.

Breaking the Code

Hard g

Ask a volunteer to read aloud the rule about **hard g.** Read the words *girl, tiger,* and *frog* aloud, emphasizing the **hard g** sound.

Read the directions for the activity aloud. Discuss the first sentence. If students are having difficulty, read the sentence and answer choices aloud, exaggerating the **hard g** sound. Have students complete the second sentence independently.

Soft g

Ask a volunteer to read aloud the rule about **soft g.** Use *judge* as an example of a word in which a silent *e* helps to make the **soft g** sound. Use *giraffe* as an example of a word in which *g* followed by *i* makes the **soft g** sound. Use *gym* as an example of a word in which *g* followed by a *y* makes the **soft g** sound.

Read the directions for the activity aloud. Discuss the third sentence. If students are having difficulty, read the sentence and answer choices aloud, exaggerating the **soft g** sound. Have students complete the fourth sentence independently.

Have students complete sentences five through eight independently.

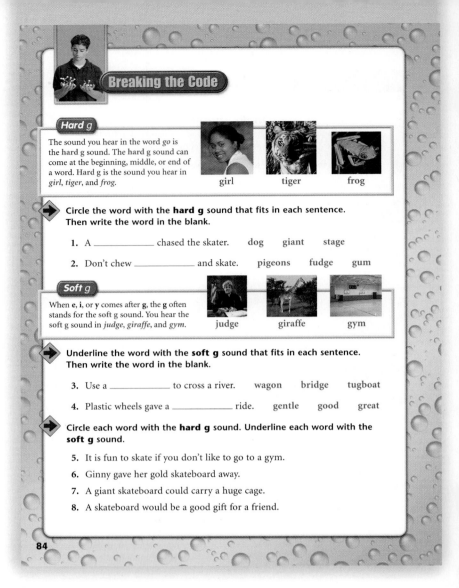

Breaking the Code

Hard g

The sound you hear in the word *go* is the hard g sound. The hard g sound can come at the beginning, middle, or end of a word. Hard g is the sound you hear in *girl, tiger,* and *frog.*

girl   tiger   frog

Circle the word with the **hard g** sound that fits in each sentence. Then write the word in the blank.

1. A _____ chased the skater.   dog   giant   stage

2. Don't chew _____ and skate.   pigeons   fudge   gum

Soft g

When **e, i,** or **y** comes after **g**, the **g** often stands for the soft g sound. You hear the soft g sound in *judge, giraffe,* and *gym.*

judge   giraffe   gym

Underline the word with the **soft g** sound that fits in each sentence. Then write the word in the blank.

3. Use a _____ to cross a river.   wagon   bridge   tugboat

4. Plastic wheels gave a _____ ride.   gentle   good   great

Circle each word with the **hard g** sound. Underline each word with the **soft g** sound.

5. It is fun to skate if you don't like to go to a gym.

6. Ginny gave her gold skateboard away.

7. A giant skateboard could carry a huge cage.

8. A skateboard would be a good gift for a friend.

84

Answers to Breaking the Code

1. (dog)

2. (gum)

3. **bridge**

4. **gentle**

5. (go) **gym**

6. Ginny (gave) (gold)

7. **giant** **huge** **cage**

8. (good) (gift)

RETEACHING

Have students re-read the selection, circling each *g* they can find. Discuss the different sounds *g* can make and have students put them into groups of words that make the same *g* sound.

Words, Words, Words

Word Endings

A suffix is an ending that changes the meaning of a word. The word *thankful* has the suffix *-ful*, and the word *slowest* has the suffix *-est*. A suffix changes the way a word is used.

➤ **Read the sentences in the box. See how the word in purple changes when a suffix is added. Adding *-ly* at the end of a word tells how something is done.**

> I made a sharp turn to the left on my skateboard.
>
> I turned sharply to the left on my skateboard.

➤ **The words in dark print below can complete the sentences. Just add the suffix *-ly* to each word and write the new word on the correct line.**

smooth   quick   safe   loud   slow

1. Metal wheels banged _____ along sidewalks.

2. Soft, plastic wheels helped skaters ride more _____.

3. If you ride a skateboard instead of walking, you can get somewhere _____.

4. Wearing a helmet will help you ride _____.

5. Skating _____ will not give you a very exciting ride.

85

Answers to Words, Words, Words

1. loudly
2. smoothly
3. quickly
4. safely
5. slowly

Words, Words, Words

Explain that a suffix is an ending that changes the meaning of a word.

Write the following three sentences on the board:

I care about my job.

I was careful.

I did the job carefully.

Ask a volunteer to read the last two sentences. **Say,** *The suffix* -ful *changed* care *into a word that means full of care. The suffix* -ly *changed* careful *into a word that tells how something was done.* Ask students to look through newspaper or magazine articles or books to find more examples of words with suffixes.

Have students complete the Word Endings activity.

RETEACHING

Write the following suffixes on the board:

-less

-ness

-ful

-ly

-y

Tell students that each of these is a suffix that can be added to a base word or root word. Have students generate a list of words that end with these suffixes. Then have them write down what the base word is without the suffix. Have students try to come up with base words that can be used with more than one of the suffixes.

REINFORCING THE THEME

To reinforce the theme, *Choose a Challenge,* have students think about a problem they helped solve. It could be a personal problem, a friend's problem, or a problem in their community. On a piece of paper, have students write "The Problem" on the left side and "The Solution" on the right side. Then have students describe the problem and solution. Tell students the story they will read is about three friends who solve a problem.

STRATEGY FOCUS

Identifying facts and opinions

Strategy

IDENTIFYING FACTS AND OPINIONS

Facts can be proved to be true. Opinions tell someone's thoughts or feelings and cannot be proved. Being able to distinguish between facts and opinions is essential for drawing conclusions from and evaluating texts.

To distinguish between facts and opinions, readers can think about the following clues:

- Facts can be checked and proven to be true.

- Opinions often use words like *think, feel, best,* or *worst.*

The activities in this unit will help students identify facts and opinions.

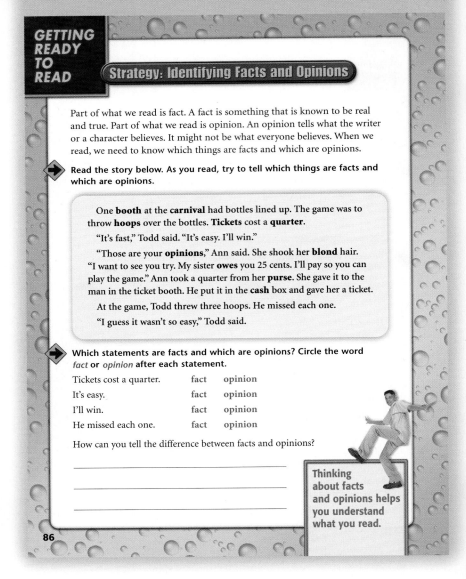

Strategy: Identifying Facts and Opinions

Part of what we read is fact. A fact is something that is known to be real and true. Part of what we read is opinion. An opinion tells what the writer or a character believes. It might not be what everyone believes. When we read, we need to know which things are facts and which are opinions.

➡ **Read the story below. As you read, try to tell which things are facts and which are opinions.**

> One **booth** at the **carnival** had bottles lined up. The game was to throw **hoops** over the bottles. **Tickets** cost a **quarter**.
>
> "It's fast," Todd said. "It's easy. I'll win."
>
> "Those are your **opinions**," Ann said. She shook her **blond** hair. "I want to see you try. My sister **owes** you 25 cents. I'll pay so you can play the game." Ann took a quarter from her **purse**. She gave it to the man in the ticket booth. He put it in the **cash** box and gave her a ticket.
>
> At the game, Todd threw three hoops. He missed each one.
>
> "I guess it wasn't so easy," Todd said.

➡ **Which statements are facts and which are opinions? Circle the word** *fact* **or** *opinion* **after each statement.**

Tickets cost a quarter.	fact	opinion
It's easy.	fact	opinion
I'll win.	fact	opinion
He missed each one.	fact	opinion

How can you tell the difference between facts and opinions?

_____

_____

_____

Thinking about facts and opinions helps you understand what you read.

86

INTRODUCING THE STRATEGY

Have students read the story. Then have them identify the facts and opinions in the story. Have students:

- think about which sentences could be proved to be true. These are facts.

- think about which sentences might be someone's belief or might not be true. These are opinions.

Explain to students that they will use this strategy as they read the story.

Note: The boldface words on this page are vocabulary words.

The words in the box come from the story you just read. You will see these words again in the story you are about to read.

booth
hoops
owes
carnival
tickets
opinions
blond
quarter
purse
cash

Complete each sentence with one of the words.

1. The team threw balls through the ___hoops___ .

2. Sara _____ her sister five dollars.

3. The _____ has rides, games, and lots of food.

4. The boy's _____ hair was so light that it looked almost white.

5. Gum costs 25 cents, so James paid with a _____ .

6. The _____ box only has four dollars in it.

7. Jeff bought two _____ to see the baseball game tonight.

8. I have _____ about baseball. I think it is a good game, but it lasts too long.

9. Sara carries her money in her _____ .

10. Jan is working in the food _____ at the baseball game.

Purpose for Reading

Now you are going to read about a crime that takes place at a carnival. As you read, think about what is fact and what is opinion.

87

Vocabulary Builder

Students are introduced to vocabulary words from the story. Reading the words in context and using them in the activity will help students comprehend the words when they read them in the story. For additional reinforcement, the vocabulary words are defined in footnotes throughout the story.

Assessment

Check students' comprehension by having each student write ten sentences—one sentence for each word—setting the word in context.

- **blond**
- **booth**
- **carnival**
- **cash**
- **hoops**
- **opinions**
- **owes**
- **purse**
- **quarter**
- **tickets**

Answers to Vocabulary Builder

1. **The first answer is provided for students. hoops**
2. **owes**
3. **carnival**
4. **blond**
5. **quarter**
6. **cash**
7. **tickets**
8. **opinions**
9. **purse**
10. **booth**

VOCABULARY EXTENSION

Write the vocabulary words on the board. Have students group together related words. Also have them explain why they grouped those words. If students have trouble, suggest that they group together words that relate to money and words that relate to carnivals. If students grouped the words in a different way, have them share the ways that they grouped the words. Discuss whether any words did not fit into any groups.

Gone!

SELECTION AT A GLANCE

Three friends, Cruz, Josie, and Ricky, are at the school carnival to raise money for a band trip when the cash box is stolen. Will they solve the crime?

INTERESTING FACTS

Many books have been published with young detectives as the protagonists. Popular series such as those about Nancy Drew, the Hardy Boys, Sammy Keyes, Herculeah Jones, Encyclopedia Brown, or the Boxcar Children have captivated young readers.

Gone!

"That prize is going to be mine," Cruz Garcia said.

His sister Josie wasn't so sure.

"I've been working at this game **booth** all morning," she told her brother. "So far, no one has won."

"Give me those **hoops**," Cruz said.

Josie took his money and handed him three hoops.

booth (BOOTH) *noun* A booth is a small building at a fair where you can play a game or buy food.
hoops (HOOPS) *noun* Hoops are large rings or circles that are sometimes made of plastic.

88

Before Reading

INTRODUCING THE SELECTION

Tell readers that they can act like detectives as they read this story. Ask them to share other detective stories they are familiar with. Discuss the kinds of details detectives look for to solve crimes. Tell them that a crime is going to occur in the story they will read and to pay attention to the details that might help solve the crime.

During Reading

PURPOSE FOR READING

Students read to learn more about the crime at the carnival and to distinguish between the facts and opinions that might help solve the crime.

APPLYING THE STRATEGY

Have students read the selection "Gone!". Remind them that they will answer Think-Along questions while they read the selection. Also remind them that answering these questions will help them distinguish between facts and opinions.

Notes

"You have to get all three over a bottle to win a prize, you know," she said.

"Watch me," Cruz said.

He threw the first hoop. It fell over the neck of a bottle, as easy as saying hello.

"Sweet," said Cruz.

Josie shook her head. That Cruz! How did he do it? Her brother's second hoop knocked into a bottle, then flew sideways.

"Sweet," joked Josie. Then, she watched with her mouth open as the hoop landed over the neck of another bottle.

"See?" Cruz said. "Nothing can stop me!"

1. What does Cruz mean when he says nothing can stop him? Write what you think.

He held up the third hoop. A little kid bumped into him just as he threw it. The hoop fell short.

"You missed," Josie said.

"Where's that kid?" Cruz said. "He **owes** me game money."

"What kid?" Josie joked.

She and Cruz looked out at the crowd that had come to the school **carnival**. Game booths and food booths lined the parking lot. Rides filled the playing field.

"We've got a good crowd for the carnival," Cruz said. "People keep coming in, like flies to honey."

---

owes (OHZ) *verb* Someone who owes something has to pay it back.
carnival (KAHR nuh vuhl) *noun* A carnival is a fair with games, rides, and food.

89

Question 1

He thinks he is going to win.

This response shows the student is thinking about the story.

He is wrong—the kid stops him!

This student has read ahead and found the answer in the next paragraph. Don't discourage this as a reading strategy, but do encourage the student to think about the question. **Say,** *Did Cruz think that was going to happen?*

MEETING INDIVIDUAL NEEDS

If students are having difficulty comprehending the selection, engage those students who may have trouble reading silently by encouraging the class to act out the story. Assign different students to be different characters. Model for them how to read in character, with changes in tone, tempo, and intonation.

"Washington, D.C., here we come!" Josie said.

Josie and Cruz both played in the school band. The band needed money for a trip to D.C., and the carnival would help pay for it.

2. Is it a fact or Josie's wish that they will have enough money to go to Washington, D.C.? Tell why you think that.

"Where's Ricky?" Josie asked.

Ricky Flores was Cruz's best friend.

"That's what I'd like to know," Cruz said. "We wanted to sell **tickets** for the rides, but they only let teachers handle the money. I don't know what Ricky's doing, but they're making me help run the Merry-Go-Round. I think that stinks!"

"Tell me how you really feel," said Josie.

Her brother was full of **opinions**, and they were all loud.

3. Does Josie agree with her brother's opinions? Tell why you think that.

---

tickets (TIHK ihts) *noun* Tickets are pieces of paper that you buy to be allowed to do something.

opinions (uh PIHN yuhnz) *noun* Opinions are what people think or believe about something.

90

Possible Responses

Question 2

It is a fact if they have it.

This student demonstrates an understanding of the nature of a fact: if a statement can be proved to be true, then it is a fact. However, the text so far does not indicate whether they have enough money. **Say,** *Do they have enough money already?*

Our band sold candy.

While this response does not answer the question, it shows the student is connecting with the story. Do not discourage this kind of personal response. **Say,** *Did you make enough for your trip? Do you think Josie's band has made enough for its trip?*

A young woman with short **blond** hair and big teeth stopped at Josie's booth. She looked at the prizes on the back wall.

"I want that turtle," the woman said.

She gave Josie a **quarter**, and Josie handed her three hoops.

The woman missed on her first try. She threw the other hoops down and walked away.

"Hey, I'll win a turtle for you," Cruz called. "I'm the best!"

The woman didn't look back.

"What's up with her?" Cruz asked.

"Who knows?" Josie said. "Maybe she's afraid of clowns."

She nodded at a tall clown dancing toward them. He had sunglasses, green hair, and a tiny red cap. A clown in a silver cape followed him, then a clown in a bird suit. A bunch of little kids followed them, shouting and laughing.

Suddenly, Josie was tired of the booth.

"My time must be up," she said. "When can I get out of here?"

"Right now," said a deep voice. A teacher she knew ducked into the booth. "My turn," he said. "Go out there and have a good time."

He didn't have to tell her twice. Josie joined Cruz in the hot Texas sun.

"Let's find Ricky," Cruz said. "I'll bet he's at the Fun House. I heard it has moving floors."

---

blond (BLAHND) *adjective* Blond is a hair color that is very light.
quarter (KWAWRT uhr) *noun* A quarter is a coin that is worth 25 cents.

91

Have students come up with examples of idiomatic or figurative language in English. Provide examples to get students started: *as hungry as a bear* or *couch potato*. Guess how the expressions might have originated. Have students translate some examples of idiomatic or figurative language from their first languages. Tell students that later they will complete an activity using figurative language from the story.

RECIPROCAL TEACHING

Clarify

Model for students how you clarify your understanding of an unknown word or a phrase. Read this sentence from the story: *A teacher she knew ducked into the booth.* Tell students that you could first understand the word *ducked* by looking at the context. Josie was waiting for someone to come in and this teacher did, so *ducked* must mean *came in*. Next, model looking the word up in a dictionary to find its exact meaning.

Have students identify words or phrases that they found confusing. Have them first use context and then look up the word in a dictionary or the glossary.

Question 3

Maybe, but she doesn't say them out loud.

This response shows a student who is comprehending as he or she reads.

Would you?

Responding with a question or with brief notes rather than in a complete sentence is appropriate. However, this response does not clearly demonstrate what the student thinks about the text. **Say,** *Do you agree with Cruz's opinions? What in the story makes you think Josie does or does not agree?*

After Reading

Have different students share their responses aloud to emphasize the many possible responses to the Think-Along questions in the boxes.

DISCUSSING THE RESPONSES

- Call on different students to share their responses.
- Have students explain what part of the story they were thinking about when they wrote.

RETEACHING

If students are having difficulty, explain to them that the Think-Along boxes are to help them think along while they read.

Choose a story the class is familiar with and model the way you think along as you read. Say aloud when the story makes you predict, compare, or use background knowledge. Point out instances when you notice the main idea, details, or facts and opinions.

Loud shouts came from somewhere near the rides.

"What's that?" Josie asked.

She and Cruz made their way through the crowd. A woman near the Wild Train Ride was shouting, "Stop him! He has my **purse**!" Her dark hair flew around her face. Something flashed as she turned her head.

"I'll get him!" cried Cruz. "Where did he go?"

The woman pointed. Josie saw something red stuck to the woman's arm. Cruz took off, and so did a crowd of kids, parents, and clowns.

Something made Josie stay back and watch. She turned around slowly, hoping to see a running man. By the time she'd turned all the way around, the woman had gone.

> 4. Why do you think the woman left after she yelled that her purse was gone?

"What's up with that?" Josie asked herself.

Then, she saw another sign of trouble. Mrs. Jackson, the teacher who had been selling tickets for the rides, had jumped to her feet. Her eyes were wide and angry.

"The **cash** box!" she cried. "The money! It's gone!"

purse (PURS) *noun* A purse is a small bag for carrying money and other things.
cash (KASH) *adjective* Cash is money in bills and coins.

92

Assessment

Informal Assessment
To assess students' understanding, use their written responses in the Think-Along boxes and their oral explanations for what they wrote.

Student Self-Assessment
Encourage students to think about their own reading experience by responding to this question: *How did answering the questions in the boxes help you think about what you read?*

Possible Responses

Question 4

She's probably looking for the guy.

Although the story later proves this response incorrect, this response makes a valid inference at this point in the story. **Say,** *That is a good guess. Let's keep reading to see what happens.*

I bet she is up to something.

This response draws a conclusion that is supported by the text and demonstrates thoughtful reading.

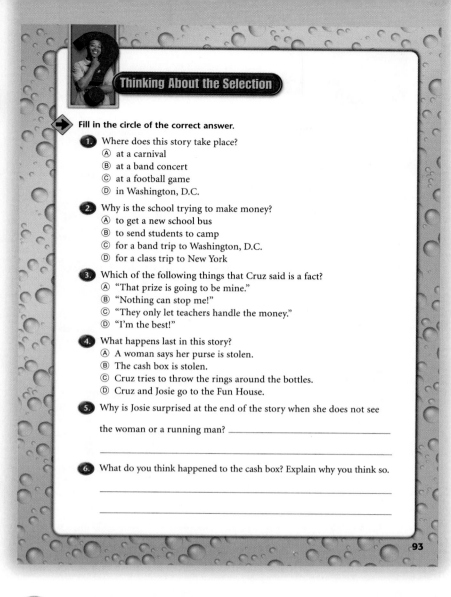

Thinking About the Selection

Fill in the circle of the correct answer.

1. Where does this story take place?
   A at a carnival
   B at a band concert
   C at a football game
   D in Washington, D.C.

2. Why is the school trying to make money?
   A to get a new school bus
   B to send students to camp
   C for a band trip to Washington, D.C.
   D for a class trip to New York

3. Which of the following things that Cruz said is a fact?
   A "That prize is going to be mine."
   B "Nothing can stop me!"
   C "They only let teachers handle the money."
   D "I'm the best!"

4. What happens last in this story?
   A A woman says her purse is stolen.
   B The cash box is stolen.
   C Cruz tries to throw the rings around the bottles.
   D Cruz and Josie go to the Fun House.

5. Why is Josie surprised at the end of the story when she does not see

   the woman or a running man? _____

   _____

6. What do you think happened to the cash box? Explain why you think so.

   _____

   _____

93

Notes

Thinking About the Selection

Explain that answering these questions will help students check their comprehension and also help them practice for other reading tests.

Have students answer the questions. Explain that, as on other tests, each multiple-choice question has one right answer, but the last two questions can be answered in different ways.

Answers to Thinking About the Selection

1. *A. at a carnival* (Literal—Setting)
2. *C. for a band trip to Washington, D.C.* (Literal—Details/Plot)
3. *C. "They only let teachers handle the money."* (Inferential—Fact/Opinion)
4. *B. The cash box is stolen.* (Literal—Sequence/Plot)
5. Accept all reasonable responses, including: *She thought the man who stole the purse would be running away.* (Inferential—Details/Plot)
6. Accept all reasonable responses, including: *The same man stole it, too.* (Inferential—Prediction/Plot)

READING LINKS

Students who enjoyed "Gone!" might want to read the entire book, *The Case of the Carnival Cash*. Students might also enjoy other mysteries.

Reading Aloud

- *The Amusement Park Mystery* by Gertrude Chandler Warner (Albert Whitman, 1991). [F]
- *The Case of the Firecrackers* by Laurence Yep (HarperCollins, Inc., 1999). [F]
- *Mysteries of People and Places* by Phyllis Raybin Emert (Tom Doherty, 1992). [NF]

Independent Reading

- *The Absent Author* by Ron Roy (Random House, 1997). [F]
- *The Animal Shelter Mystery* by Gertrude Chandler Warner (Albert Whitman, 1991). [F]
- *Cam Jansen and the Mystery of the Carnival Prize* by David Adler (Viking Penguin, 1998). [F]
- *Snowbound Mystery* by Gertrude Chandler Warner (Albert Whitman, 1990). [F]

FAMILY INVOLVEMENT

Have each student ask an adult family member this question: *If there was one thing that you could make sure I never do, what would it be and why?* The student and adult should talk about why this advice is important. Volunteers can then share the advice they gained with classmates.

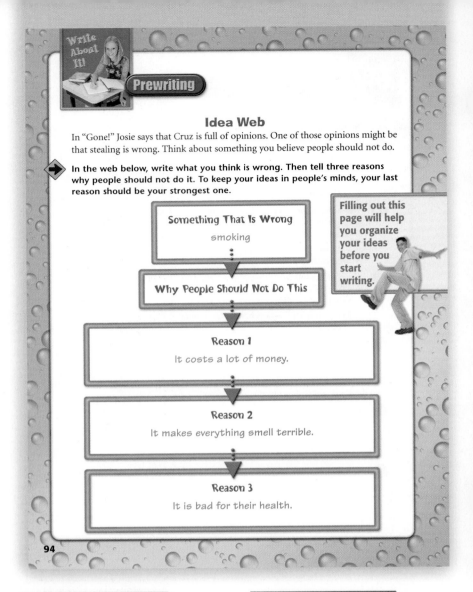

Idea Web

In "Gone!" Josie says that Cruz is full of opinions. One of those opinions might be that stealing is wrong. Think about something you believe people should not do.

In the web below, write what you think is wrong. Then tell three reasons why people should not do it. To keep your ideas in people's minds, your last reason should be your strongest one.

Filling out this page will help you organize your ideas before you start writing.

Something That Is Wrong
smoking

Why People Should Not Do This

Reason 1
It costs a lot of money.

Reason 2
It makes everything smell terrible.

Reason 3
It is bad for their health.

94

Before Writing

Have students brainstorm things that are harmful or hurtful to others. Write these ideas on the board. If students are having trouble generating ideas, talk to them about what makes some behaviors wrong. Say, *What is something that makes you mad or upset when you see someone doing it? Why is this thing so wrong?*

Or, have students write in journals to brainstorm ideas before they begin working independently on their webs.

During Writing

Have students refer to their webs. Personalize the experience for students having difficulty. Say, *What do you hate to see your friends or family do? What would you tell them to get them to stop?*

A Plan for Writing

In My Opinion, This Is Wrong

A persuasive essay tells an opinion. The writer tries to get people to think or feel a certain way. The essay must list good reasons to help people change their minds.

➡ **Write a plan for a persuasive essay to tell people why they should not do something. Use ideas from your idea web.**

Tell what is wrong.

Smoking _____ is wrong. There are three reasons why people should not do this.

Explain the first reason.

People should not smoke _____ because cigarettes cost a lot of money when they keep buying them. That money could be spent on something fun or healthy.

Explain the second reason.

People also should not smoke _____ because it makes everything smell terrible. The bad smell stays on clothes and hair for a long time.

Explain the last reason.

The last reason people should not smoke _____ is because it's bad for their health. It causes disease and death. It is also dangerous for everyone around the smoker.

Writing

➡ **Write a persuasive essay to tell people your opinion. Tell what is wrong and why people should not do it. You can give more details, but use the same order as your plan. Save your strongest reason for last. Write your essay on a sheet of paper.**

95

After Writing

Discuss students' reactions to what they have written. Ask students whether their classmates had pointed out any behaviors that they should change. Have students reflect in journals on how they might change as a result of other students' writing.

GROUP SHARING

Pair students to read each other's essays. Have the partners try to argue against each other's points. Have some pairs debate their positions in front of the class.

Assessment

Portfolio Assessment
Students may want to save their persuasive essays in their classroom portfolios.

Student Self-Assessment
Encourage students to think about their writing experience. **Say,** *How did writing to get other people to change their behavior help you think about your own? Is there anything you would change?*

SCORING RUBRIC: PERSUASIVE ESSAY

SCORE 3
Essay is persuasive. Topic is clearly defined and supporting details are well developed. Contains clear, vivid sensory details. Writing is organized and coherent. Contains few errors in sentence structure, usage, mechanics, or spelling.

SCORE 2
Essay is persuasive. Topic is defined and supporting ideas are developed. Contains sensory details, but some are not vivid; some may not be clear. Has some degree of organization and coherence. Contains some errors in sentence structure, usage, mechanics, or spelling.

SCORE 1
Essay is not persuasive. Topic is not clearly defined or supporting details are weak. Writing contains few or no sensory details and most are not vivid or clear. Has minimal organization and coherence. Contains many errors in sentence structure, usage, mechanics, or spelling.

Breaking the Code

Hard c

Ask a volunteer to read aloud the rule about **hard c.** Read the words *cat, car,* and *clam* aloud, emphasizing the **hard c** sound.

Read the directions for the activity aloud and discuss the first sentence. If students are having difficulty, read the sentence and answer choices aloud, exaggerating the **hard c** sound. Have students complete the second sentence independently.

Soft c

Ask a volunteer to read aloud the rule about **soft c.** Use *cent* as an example of a word in which *c* followed by *e* makes the **soft c** sound. Use *city* as an example of a word in which *c* followed by *i* makes the **soft c** sound. Use *bicycle* as an example of a word in which *c* followed by *y* makes the **soft c** sound.

Read the directions for the activity aloud. Discuss the third sentence. If students are having difficulty, read the sentence and answer choices aloud, exaggerating the **soft c** sound. Have students complete the fourth sentence independently.

Have students complete sentences five through eight independently.

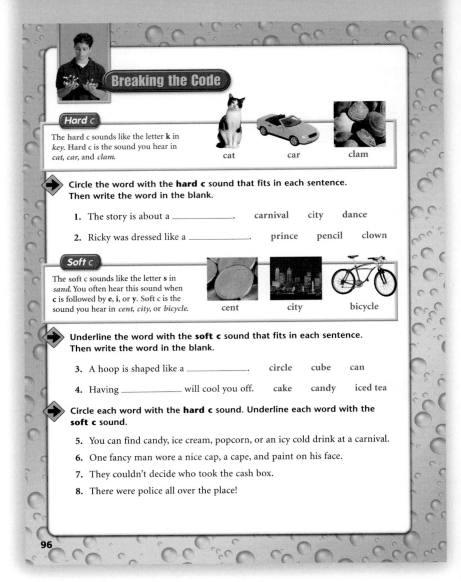

Breaking the Code

Hard c

The hard c sounds like the letter **k** in *key.* Hard c is the sound you hear in *cat, car,* and *clam.*

cat   car   clam

➡ Circle the word with the **hard c** sound that fits in each sentence. Then write the word in the blank.

1. The story is about a _____.   carnival   city   dance
2. Ricky was dressed like a _____.   prince   pencil   clown

Soft c

The soft c sounds like the letter **s** in *sand.* You often hear this sound when c is followed by **e, i,** or **y.** Soft c is the sound you hear in *cent, city,* or *bicycle.*

cent   city   bicycle

➡ Underline the word with the **soft c** sound that fits in each sentence. Then write the word in the blank.

3. A hoop is shaped like a _____.   circle   cube   can
4. Having _____ will cool you off.   cake   candy   iced tea

➡ Circle each word with the **hard c** sound. Underline each word with the **soft c** sound.

5. You can find candy, ice cream, popcorn, or an icy cold drink at a carnival.
6. One fancy man wore a nice cap, a cape, and paint on his face.
7. They couldn't decide who took the cash box.
8. There were police all over the place!

96

Answers to Breaking the Code

1. (carnival)
2. (clown)
3. circle
4. iced tea
5. (can) (candy) ice (cream) (popcorn) icy (cold) (carnival)
6. fancy nice (cap) (cape) face
7. (couldn't) decide (cash)
8. police place

RETEACHING

Divide the class into four groups. Have the first group generate words with a **soft c** that describe places you can go (such as *city*). Have the second group generate words with a **hard c** that describe people or animals (such as *clown* or *cat*). Have the third group generate words with a **soft c** that describe things you can do (such as *race*). Have the last group generate words with a **hard c** that describe actions (such as *carry*). Give the groups ten minutes to generate their word lists. Then have them share the results with the class.

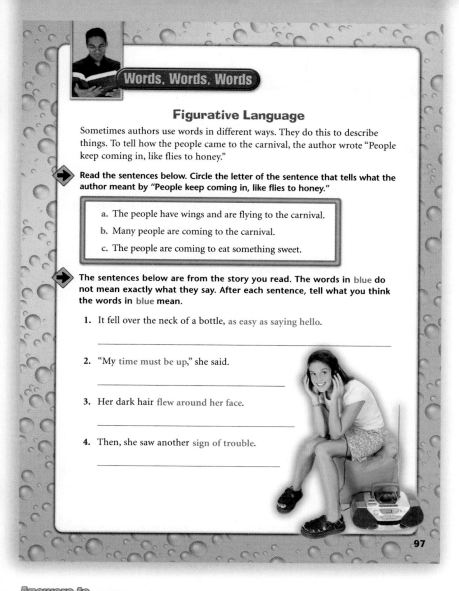

Words, Words, Words

Figurative Language

Sometimes authors use words in different ways. They do this to describe things. To tell how the people came to the carnival, the author wrote "People keep coming in, like flies to honey."

➤ Read the sentences below. Circle the letter of the sentence that tells what the author meant by "People keep coming in, like flies to honey."

  a. The people have wings and are flying to the carnival.

  b. Many people are coming to the carnival.

  c. The people are coming to eat something sweet.

➤ The sentences below are from the story you read. The words in blue do not mean exactly what they say. After each sentence, tell what you think the words in blue mean.

1. It fell over the neck of a bottle, as easy as saying hello.

   _____

2. "My time must be up," she said.

   _____

3. Her dark hair flew around her face.

   _____

4. Then, she saw another sign of trouble.

   _____

97

Answers to Words, Words, Words

1. Answers will vary. Accept responses like: *easily* or *smoothly*

2. Answers will vary. Accept responses like: *time is over*

3. Answers will vary. Accept responses like: *was moving around her face*

4. Answers will vary. Accept responses like: *problem*

Words, Words, Words

Explain that authors often use words in different ways to describe people, things, or actions and to create clearer pictures in their readers' minds.

Discuss this example with the class. In the story, Cruz says he thinks it "stinks" that he has to run the Merry-Go-Round instead of selling tickets. What does Cruz mean by "stinks"? Elicit the response that "stinks" does not literally mean smells bad, but that Cruz used "stinks" to mean unfair or bad.

Have students complete the Figurative Language activity.

RETEACHING

Explain to students that authors use figurative language to describe things in unusual ways. Often, they compare two unlike things to bring a more vivid picture to the reader's mind. Have students think about what is being compared in the examples from the story. Have them think about what is being described. Then have them rewrite the sentences using their own figurative language. Model an example for them, using the sample sentence. "People keep coming in, like flies to honey" could become "People keep coming in, *like ants to our picnic.*"

Have students look for examples of figurative language in other books that they are reading.

REINFORCING THE THEME

To reinforce the theme, *Choose a Challenge,* have students think about a job or activity they would like to do when they are older. What steps could they take toward making it happen? On a sheet of paper, have students write "What I'd like to do when I'm older" on the left side and "What I'll need to do to make it happen" on the right side. Have them write their thoughts below. Tell students the story they will read is about a man who wanted to entertain people and how he was able to do so.

STRATEGY FOCUS

Identifying facts and opinions

Strategy

IDENTIFYING FACTS AND OPINIONS

Facts can be proved to be true. Opinions tell thoughts or feelings that may be true to one person but not to another. Distinguishing between facts and opinions is crucial for comprehension.

Encourage readers to:

- think about the author or the source of information, and
- think about whether the information can be proved.

The activities in this unit will help students apply the strategy of identifying facts and opinions.

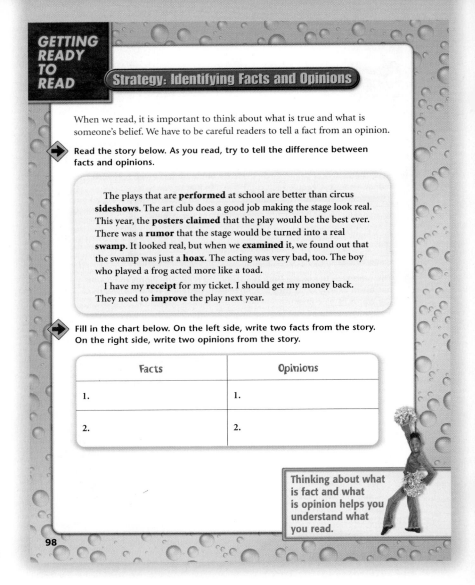

GETTING
READY
TO
READ **Strategy: Identifying Facts and Opinions**

When we read, it is important to think about what is true and what is someone's belief. We have to be careful readers to tell a fact from an opinion.

➡ Read the story below. As you read, try to tell the difference between facts and opinions.

The plays that are **performed** at school are better than circus **sideshows**. The art club does a good job making the stage look real. This year, the **posters claimed** that the play would be the best ever. There was a **rumor** that the stage would be turned into a real **swamp**. It looked real, but when we **examined** it, we found out that the swamp was just a **hoax**. The acting was very bad, too. The boy who played a frog acted more like a toad.

I have my **receipt** for my ticket. I should get my money back. They need to **improve** the play next year.

➡ Fill in the chart below. On the left side, write two facts from the story. On the right side, write two opinions from the story.

Facts	Opinions
1.	1.
2.	2.

Thinking about what is fact and what is opinion helps you understand what you read.

98

INTRODUCING THE STRATEGY

Have students read the selection, then have them identify two facts and opinions. Tell students to:

- think about which sentences are true for everyone. These are facts.
- think about which sentences might be true for only some people but not for everyone. These are opinions.

Explain to students that they will use this strategy as they read "A Star Is Born."

Note: The boldface words on this page are vocabulary words.

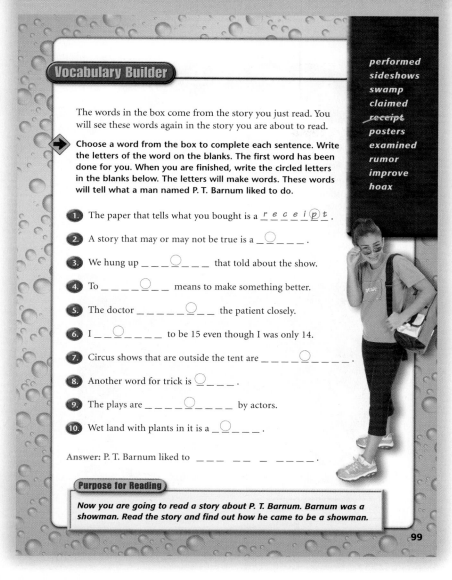

Vocabulary Builder

The words in the box come from the story you just read. You will see these words again in the story you are about to read.

performed
sideshows
swamp
claimed
receipt
posters
examined
rumor
improve
hoax

➡ Choose a word from the box to complete each sentence. Write the letters of the word on the blanks. The first word has been done for you. When you are finished, write the circled letters in the blanks below. The letters will make words. These words will tell what a man named P. T. Barnum liked to do.

1. The paper that tells what you bought is a _r_ _e_ _c_ _e_ _i_ (p) _t_ .

2. A story that may or may not be true is a _ (_) _ _ _ .

3. We hung up _ _ _ (_) _ _ _ that told about the show.

4. To _ _ _ _ (_) _ _ means to make something better.

5. The doctor _ _ _ _ _ (_) _ _ the patient closely.

6. I _ _ (_) _ _ _ to be 15 even though I was only 14.

7. Circus shows that are outside the tent are _ _ _ _ (_) _ _ _ _ .

8. Another word for trick is (_) _ _ _ .

9. The plays are _ _ _ _ (_) _ _ _ by actors.

10. Wet land with plants in it is a _ (_) _ _ _ .

Answer: P. T. Barnum liked to _ _ _   _ _   _   _ _ _ _ .

Purpose for Reading

Now you are going to read a story about P. T. Barnum. Barnum was a showman. Read the story and find out how he came to be a showman.

99

This activity introduces students to key vocabulary words in context that will support their comprehension of the selection. For additional reinforcement, the vocabulary words are defined in footnotes throughout the story.

Assessment

Check students' comprehension by having them use their own words to write a definition for each vocabulary word.

- **claimed**
- **examined**
- **hoax**
- **improve**
- **performed**
- **posters**
- **receipt**
- **rumor**
- **sideshows**
- **swamp**

Answers to Vocabulary Builder

1. **The first answer is provided for students.** recei(p)t

2. r(u)mor

3. pos(t)ers

4. impr(o)ve

5. exami(n)ed

6. cl(a)imed

7. side(s)hows

8. (h)oax

9. perf(o)rmed

10. s(w)amp

Answer: P.T. Barnum liked to **put on a show.**

Vocabulary Extension

Have students look up the words in a dictionary and compare the dictionary definitions to the definitions they wrote in their own words.

SELECTION AT A GLANCE

This selection is about the early years of P. T. Barnum, the great showman and founder of the Barnum and Bailey Circus.

INTERESTING FACTS

P. T. Barnum stood far above others as a showman. He has been called a genius at putting on a good show. Barnum also has been called the inventor of hype. His advertising gimmicks not only brought crowds of people to his shows, they set new standards for advertising and publicity. Barnum was chosen by *Life* magazine as one of the hundred most important people of the millenium.

A Star Is Born

It's Spring, and the Circus Is Here!

New York, New York, 2002 – It must be spring. The circus is in town again.

The Barnum & Bailey Circus has been around for more than 130 years. The shows used to take place in tents. Now they are **performed** indoors. Today you'll see fancy light shows. Of course, animals and people still do tricks. Sometimes there are **sideshows**. You can see the world's strongest man pull a truck. You may get to watch a man eat fire!

P. T. Barnum would have liked this circus. He always loved a good show. In fact, nobody put on a better show than P. T. Barnum.

performed (puhr FAWRMD) *adjective* To be performed means to be put on, as in an act or show.
sideshows (SYD shohz) *noun* Sideshows are circus shows that are not in the main tent.

100

Before Reading

INTRODUCING THE SELECTION

Tell readers that it can be hard to tell fact from opinion when someone is intentionally trying to mislead them. Ask students to think of a time when they thought something was a fact and then later found out it was not. It might be a time someone played a practical joke or did not tell the truth about something. Tell students that they will read about a famous joker, P. T. Barnum.

During Reading

PURPOSE FOR READING

Students read to learn more about P. T. Barnum.

APPLYING THE STRATEGY

Have students read the selection "A Star Is Born." Remind them that they will answer Think-Along questions while they read the selection. Explain that answering these questions will help them distinguish between facts and opinions.

Notes

Small Boy Likes Big Joke

Bethel, Connecticut, 1821 – P. T. Barnum thought he was the richest 11-year-old boy in town until yesterday.

P. T.'s grandfather gave him Ivy Island when he was born on July 5, 1810. P. T.'s family always told him how lucky he was. Neighbors said that Ivy Island was one of the best farms in Connecticut.

P. T. had never seen his island. Finally, his family agreed that he should see it. P. T. was in for a surprise.

Yesterday, P. T. explored Ivy Island. It was not a fun adventure. P. T. stumbled into a **swamp** and stepped on a bee's nest. Then a snake came after him. Ivy Island was a terrible place.

Young P. T. knows that he was tricked, but he says that he always likes a good joke. P. T. tells us that his grandfather is more fun than anyone he knows. One day, P. T. hopes to be just like him.

> 1. Why wasn't young Barnum upset with his grandfather for playing the trick on him? Write what you think.

Barnum's 160-Year-Old Woman

New York, New York, 1835 – Mr. P. T. Barnum has opened a show here in New York City. People can't wait to meet the 160-year-old woman in his show. How in the world did Barnum find her?

Mr. Barnum was working in his store one day last summer. A friend stopped by to visit. He described a show that he wanted to sell. The show starred a 160-year-old woman. Barnum was interested. He decided to go meet Joice Heth, the 160-year-old woman.

swamp (SWAHMP) *noun* A swamp is a piece of wet land that is full of mud, water, and plants.

101

Select five theme-related words or five words from the story with which students will likely be unfamiliar. Write the correct definitions for the words on index cards. Divide the class into three teams. Have each team write a false definition for each word on an index card.

Read the one correct and three false definitions for each word. Have students guess which definition is correct. Discuss what clues helped students guess which was the correct definition.

NONFICTION READING STRATEGY

Research Skills

Encourage students to keep a list of words they don't recognize as they read. Have them jot down any context clues or guesses about the meaning of the word on the same sheet of paper. When students are finished reading, encourage them to look the words up in the dictionary and write the dictionary definition next to their own notes.

Question 1

He said he likes a good joke.

This response shows the student is thinking while reading. The response has a direct connection with the text.

If you are that kind of person then you won't be mad.

This response suggests that the student is connecting with the text. **Say,** *Tell me more about what you mean by "that kind of person."*

If students are having difficulty comprehending the selection, encourage them to make a web to organize the details they learn about P. T. Barnum. Write *P. T. Barnum* inside a circle. Then, in spokes coming from the circle, write facts, details, or opinions learned from the selection.

Barnum described Miss Heth as a tiny lady. Her face looked as rough and dry as an elephant's. The old lady could barely move. She also had no teeth, and she couldn't see.

Miss Heth **claimed** that she had taken care of George Washington when he was a boy. She told Barnum stories about "dear little George." Miss Heth also showed Barnum a **receipt** from 1727. The receipt showed that George Washington's father had bought her to be a slave.

2. What could Barnum have asked for that would prove that Miss Heth was 160 years old?

Barnum was thrilled by Miss Heth, so he bought the show. He hung up **posters** on the streets. Soon crowds were lining up to see her.

The crowds keep coming. Barnum says he loves entertaining them. Ah, what a life!

claimed (KLAYMD) *verb* Claimed means said something that you believed was true or wanted others to believe.
receipt (rih SEET) *noun* A receipt is a piece of paper that you get when you buy something.
posters (POHS tuhrz) *noun* Posters are big pieces of paper covered by pictures and words.

102

Question 2

license

A one-word response to a Think-Along question is acceptable. In discussion, encourage the student to explain the connection with the text. **Say,** *Tell me more about what you wrote.*

I don't know.

Encourage this student to try to answer the question. **Say,** *How could you prove how old you are?*

The Truth About the 161-Year-Old Woman

Philadelphia, Pennsylvania, Feb. 19, 1836 – Joice Heth died today. Doctors have **examined** her body. They say that she was only about 80 years old. Her insides were in such good shape that she couldn't have been 161!

When P. T. Barnum learned the news, he seemed surprised. He said that he truly believed that Joice Heth was 161. Barnum claimed that he had been tricked. He pointed to his receipt from 1727. Did Barnum trick everyone, or did Barnum's friend trick him?

> 3. Do you think Barnum really thought that Miss Heth was 161 when she died? Tell why you do or do not think so.

If Barnum were playing a trick, we would not be surprised. A few months ago, Barnum took Miss Heth to Boston. A **rumor** started there that she was a machine, not a person. It was said that a man hid during the shows and spoke for the machine. Before this rumor started, ticket sales were low. Some people think that Barnum himself started the rumor to **improve** sales.

Some people believe that Barnum made up Joice Heth's story. They think that he lied about the receipt. Barnum still claims that he never lied.

---

examined (ehg ZAM uhnd) *verb* Examined means looked at something very carefully.
rumor (ROO muhr) *noun* A rumor is a story told as news and passed from person to person. A rumor may or may not be true.
improve (ihm PROOV) *verb* To improve means to make something better than it was before.

103

Students from other countries may not have been to a circus. Encourage any students who have been to a circus to share their experiences. Share your own circus stories as well. If possible, share a picture book or photos of a circus. Encourage students to ask questions.

RECIPROCAL TEACHING

Predict

Tell students that this selection is the first chapter in a longer book. Have students write a paragraph predicting what the book will tell about next.

When students have finished writing, have them share their predictions with the class. Discuss different predictions and have students support their responses with specific examples from the text.

Question 3

No because he liked a joke.

Encourage this student to elaborate further in discussion. **Say,** *What in the story made you think this?*

Why wouldn't he have believed her?

Responding with a question rather than with a sentence is appropriate. Encourage the student to try to answer his or her question. **Say,** *Why do you think he might not have believed her?*

After Reading

Have students share their responses to the questions in the Think-Along boxes and their thoughts about the reading selection.

DISCUSSING THE RESPONSES

- Ask for volunteers to share their responses.
- Have students cite specific text examples or background knowledge that made them answer as they did.
- Discuss how answering the questions helped students think about what they were reading.

RETEACHING

If students are having difficulty, do the activity with them. Share your responses to each Think-Along question and explain the connections between your responses and the text.

What is the truth? We may never know. But one thing is certain. People paid money for this big bad **hoax**. Barnum should have learned the truth about Joice Heth before he opened his show.

4. Do you think it was a fact or an opinion that Barnum made up Joice Heth's story? Tell why you think so.

hoax (HOHKS) *noun* A hoax is a trick or mean joke.

104

Assessment

Informal Assessment
Use students' written responses and their discussion to help you determine how well they comprehended as they read.

Student Self-Assessment
Encourage students to think about their own reading experience by responding to this question: *How did reading this story and answering the questions help you think about the difference between fact and opinion?*

Possible Responses

Question 4

It's an opinion because people disagreed and because no one proved it.

This response shows comprehension of the text and an understanding of the distinction between facts and opinions.

It's a fact.

Encourage this student to elaborate further in discussion. **Say,** *What in the story makes you think that it was a fact?*

104

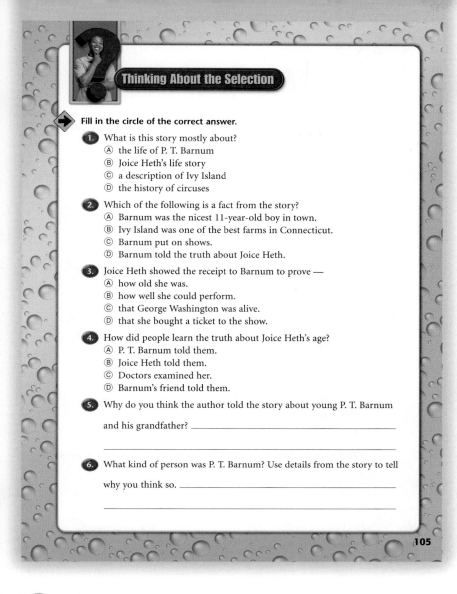

Thinking About the Selection

Fill in the circle of the correct answer.

1. What is this story mostly about?
   - Ⓐ the life of P. T. Barnum
   - Ⓑ Joice Heth's life story
   - Ⓒ a description of Ivy Island
   - Ⓓ the history of circuses

2. Which of the following is a fact from the story?
   - Ⓐ Barnum was the nicest 11-year-old boy in town.
   - Ⓑ Ivy Island was one of the best farms in Connecticut.
   - Ⓒ Barnum put on shows.
   - Ⓓ Barnum told the truth about Joice Heth.

3. Joice Heth showed the receipt to Barnum to prove —
   - Ⓐ how old she was.
   - Ⓑ how well she could perform.
   - Ⓒ that George Washington was alive.
   - Ⓓ that she bought a ticket to the show.

4. How did people learn the truth about Joice Heth's age?
   - Ⓐ P. T. Barnum told them.
   - Ⓑ Joice Heth told them.
   - Ⓒ Doctors examined her.
   - Ⓓ Barnum's friend told them.

5. Why do you think the author told the story about young P. T. Barnum and his grandfather? _____

   _____

6. What kind of person was P. T. Barnum? Use details from the story to tell why you think so. _____

   _____

105

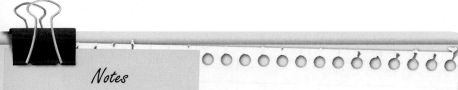

Notes

Thinking About the Selection

Explain that answering these questions will help students check their comprehension. Answering the questions will also help them practice for other reading tests.

Have students answer the questions. Explain that, as on other tests, each multiple-choice question has one right answer, but the last two questions can be answered in different ways.

Answers to Thinking About the Selection

1. **A. the life of P. T. Barnum** (Inferential—Main Idea)
2. **C. Barnum put on shows.** (Inferential Fact/Opinion)
3. **A. how old she was.** (Literal—Cause/Effect)
4. **C. Doctors examined her.** (Literal—Detail)
5. Accept all reasonable responses, including: *To show that P. T. Barnum always loved a good joke and to show where he got his love of jokes.* (Inferential— Author's Purpose)
6. Accept all reasonable responses, including: *He loved jokes and loved entertaining people, even if he had to lie to do it.* (Literal—Details)

Students who enjoyed "A Star Is Born" might want to read the entire book, *The World's Greatest Showman*. Students might also enjoy reading other biographies about both real and legendary people.

Reading Aloud

- *At Her Majesty's Request: An African Princess in Victorian England* by Walter Dean Myers (Scholastic, 1999). [NF]

- *At the Plate with Sammy Sosa* by Matt Christopher (Little, Brown, 1999). [NF]

- *Maya Angelou: Greeting the Morning* by Sarah King (Millbrook, 1994). [NF]

- *Spellbinder: The Life of Harry Houdini* by Tom Lalicki (Holiday House, 2000). [NF]

Independent Reading

- *John Henry* by Julius Lester (Putnam, 1999). [F]

- *John James Audobon* by Martha Kendall (Millbrook, 1993). [NF]

- *Building a Dream* by Richard Kelso (Steck-Vaughn, 1996). [NF]

FAMILY INVOLVEMENT

Discuss with students what constitutes a good-natured, practical joke. Give an example from your own experience. Ask students to talk with a family member about a practical joke that had been played on him or her. Volunteers can then share their stories with classmates.

Prewriting

Idea Web

In "A Star Is Born" we learned that P. T. Barnum was good at selling tickets to his shows. Think about something that people would like to see or buy. It could be real or something you make up. It could even be a hoax!

➡ **Fill in the idea web below. Tell about something you think people would see or buy. Also, tell what that thing is like.**

Something people would see or buy: a ticket to the "My Life in 20 Years" machine.

Why people should see or buy it: It lets you see your life in the future. You can see how you will look, what job you'll have, and so on.

What this thing is like: This machine has a comfortable chair and a special screen.

Filling out this page will help you organize your ideas before you start writing.

106

Before Writing

Have students brainstorm things or ideas, real or imagined, that are amazing. Write these ideas on the board. Help students who are having trouble generating ideas. **Say,** *If people could do or see anything, no matter the cost, what would it be?*

Or, have students work in small groups to brainstorm ideas before they begin working independently on their webs.

During Writing

Have students refer to their webs. Remind students to use a showman-like style in their speeches. Personalize the experience for students having difficulty. **Say,** *Why would you pay money to do or see something? What would be so great about it?*

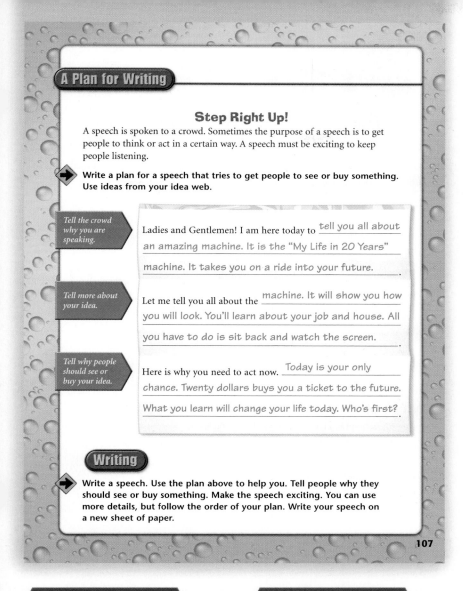

A Plan for Writing

Step Right Up!

A speech is spoken to a crowd. Sometimes the purpose of a speech is to get people to think or act in a certain way. A speech must be exciting to keep people listening.

➡ **Write a plan for a speech that tries to get people to see or buy something. Use ideas from your idea web.**

Tell the crowd why you are speaking.

Ladies and Gentlemen! I am here today to tell you all about an amazing machine. It is the "My Life in 20 Years" machine. It takes you on a ride into your future.

Tell more about your idea.

Let me tell you all about the machine. It will show you how you will look. You'll learn about your job and house. All you have to do is sit back and watch the screen.

Tell why people should see or buy your idea.

Here is why you need to act now. Today is your only chance. Twenty dollars buys you a ticket to the future. What you learn will change your life today. Who's first?

Writing

➡ **Write a speech. Use the plan above to help you. Tell people why they should see or buy something. Make the speech exciting. You can use more details, but follow the order of your plan. Write your speech on a new sheet of paper.**

107

After Writing

As a group, discuss students' reactions to what they have written. Encourage students to explore ways in which people try to sell things—and why people buy things.

GROUP SHARING

When students have finished writing, organize them into groups to compare their speeches. Have each group pick the best speech. Have the writer deliver the speech to the class, in true showman-like style.

Assessment

Portfolio Assessment
Students may want to save their speeches in their classroom portfolios.

Student Self-Assessment
Encourage students to think about their writing experience. Ask, *How is written language different from spoken language?*

SCORING RUBRIC: SPEECH

SCORE 3

Topic is clearly defined and supporting details are well developed. Contains conventions of speech and clear, vivid sensory details. Writing is organized and coherent. Contains few errors in sentence structure, usage, mechanics, or spelling.

SCORE 2

Topic is defined and supporting ideas are developed. Contains conventions of speech. Contains sensory details, but some are not vivid; some may not be clear. Has some degree of organization and coherence. Contains some errors in sentence structure, usage, mechanics, or spelling.

SCORE 1

Topic is not clearly defined or idea development is weak. Does not contain conventions of speech. Writing contains few or no sensory details and most are not vivid or clear. Has minimal organization and coherence. Contains many errors in sentence structure, usage, mechanics, or spelling.

Breaking the Code

The s sound

Ask a volunteer to read aloud the rule about the **s sound** of *s*. Read the words *dress, sock,* and *bus* aloud, emphasizing the **s sound.**

Read the directions for the activity aloud. Discuss the first sentence. If students are having difficulty, read the sentence and answer choices aloud, exaggerating the **s sound.** Have students complete the second sentence independently.

The z sound

Ask a volunteer to read aloud the rule about the **z sound** of *s*. Read the words *rose, peas,* and *cheese* aloud, emphasizing the **z sound.**

Read the directions for the activity aloud. Discuss the third sentence. If students are having difficulty, read the sentence and answer choices aloud, exaggerating the **z sound.** Have students complete the fourth sentence independently.

Have students complete sentences five through eight independently.

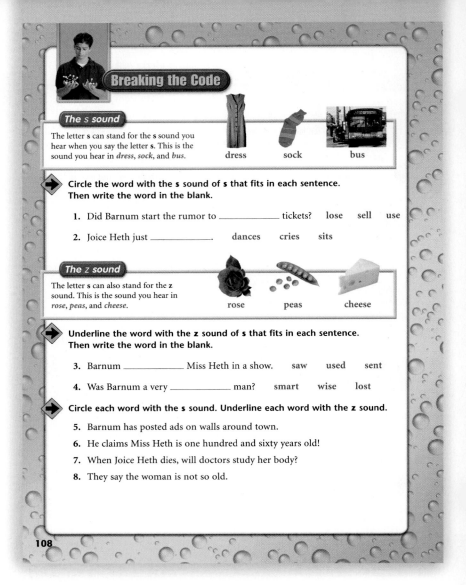

Breaking the Code

The s sound

The letter **s** can stand for the **s** sound you hear when you say the letter **s**. This is the sound you hear in *dress, sock,* and *bus.*

dress   sock   bus

➤ Circle the word with the **s** sound of **s** that fits in each sentence. Then write the word in the blank.

1. Did Barnum start the rumor to _____ tickets?   lose   sell   use

2. Joice Heth just _____.   dances   cries   sits

The z sound

The letter **s** can also stand for the **z** sound. This is the sound you hear in *rose, peas,* and *cheese.*

rose   peas   cheese

➤ Underline the word with the **z** sound of **s** that fits in each sentence. Then write the word in the blank.

3. Barnum _____ Miss Heth in a show.   saw   used   sent

4. Was Barnum a very _____ man?   smart   wise   lost

➤ Circle each word with the **s** sound. Underline each word with the **z** sound.

5. Barnum has posted ads on walls around town.

6. He claims Miss Heth is one hundred and sixty years old!

7. When Joice Heth dies, will doctors study her body?

8. They say the woman is not so old.

108

Answers to Breaking the Code

1. (sell)

2. (sits)

3. used

4. wise

5. has (posted) ads walls

6. claims (Miss) is (sixty) years

7. dies doctors (study)

8. (say) is (so)

RETEACHING

Divide the class into three groups. Have one group generate names of fruits and vegetables that have an **s** or **z** **sound.** Have the second group list names of people with an **s** or **z** **sound.** Assign the third group names of places that have an **s** or **z** **sound.** Give all groups five minutes to generate their lists. Then, have the groups switch lists twice more, giving each group five minutes to add to the previous list. Share the results with the class and discuss if there was one set of words for which it was easiest to generate ideas.

Words, Words, Words

Using Reference Materials

You use reference materials to find out about something. A dictionary is a reference book that tells:

- how to say a word
- what a word means
- how to spell a word
- what part of speech a word is

The words in a dictionary are called *entry words*. These words are listed in A-B-C order. Each meaning is numbered.

The top of each dictionary page has guide words which show the first and last word on that page. The entry words are listed in A-B-C order between the guide words.

Read the dictionary entry below. Then answer the questions.

> **show**   1. *verb* to allow to be seen
> 2. *noun* a play or concert

1. Circle the two guide words that might appear at the top of the dictionary page listing the word **show**.

   set ——— shake

   shake ——— shop

   short ——— shower

   shower —— shrink

2. How many meanings are given for the word **show**? _____

3. Which meaning is used in the sentence "It was a great show"? _____

Now, write your own sentence using the word **show**. In the box, write the number of the meaning you are using for the word **show**.

_____ _____

109

Words, Words, Words

Ask for three different volunteers to read the paragraphs at the top of the page. Discuss with students if they have any questions about the information provided.

If students are having difficulty understanding the information, model for them how to use a page from a dictionary.

Have students complete the Using Reference Materials activity. When students are finished, discuss their responses. Have them explain how they determined their answers.

RETEACHING

Either individually or in small groups, have students write a set of directions that explains how to use a dictionary. Ask students to write the directions to a younger student. Encourage students to use numbered steps, clear examples, and simple language so their directions are easy for a younger student to use.

Answers to Words, Words, Words

1. **short**   **shower**

2. **Two**

3. **2**

Answers will vary. Accept any responses that correctly use a meaning of the word *show,* such as:

1. **I will show you my house.**

or

2. **I went to a good show.**

THEME WRAP-UP SELECTIONS

There are two types of selections in this Theme Wrap-Up. This first selection is a fiction story and the second selection is a nonfiction article. These selections serve three purposes.

First, they offer another perspective on the theme *Choose a Challenge* that can be used as a basis for discussion. After your students have finished reading, you may want to engage them in a discussion or writing activity about how these selections fit into the theme *Choose a Challenge*.

Second, the selections provide another venue for using Think-Along questions and practicing some of the strategies taught in this theme. These selections are designed to show students how thinking along will help them comprehend what they are reading and better answer questions about what they have read.

Third, the selections provide models similar to reading comprehension passages on standardized tests. Each selection is followed by a set of multiple-choice and short-answer questions. The question format is typical of many standardized and criterion-referenced tests. These questions help students check comprehension and prepare them for taking standardized tests.

A Trumpet for Derek

Derek sat on the edge of his seat. He tried to see around the heads of the students in front of him. Even though he was older than all of them, he was the smallest in his class.

As he listened to the concert, Derek forgot about his sick lungs. He watched the man on stage playing a golden trumpet. The voice of the trumpet filled the room. Listening to the music made Derek feel stronger. He had never heard a prouder sound.

When the song ended, the man bowed, and everyone clapped. Derek felt sad when the man left the stage.

Back in class, Derek sat quietly. He stared out the window.

1. What do you think Derek was thinking about?

"Who was that man playing the trumpet?" he asked his teacher.

The teacher gave him a paper that listed the songs in the concert. At the bottom it said, "Chris Brook, Trumpet."

Derek gave the paper back to his teacher. He thought about the man and his shiny trumpet.

When Derek got home, he took his pills without making a face. He breathed the mist of medicine for the whole ten minutes. He didn't even fuss when it was time for his mom to thump on his back and chest. Then he turned on the computer.

"What's this?" his mom asked from the door. "You haven't frowned once since you got home."

Derek smiled. "I'm feeling good today."

His mom laughed and pushed her glasses higher on her nose. "Everyone should be so happy." She left Derek alone.

110

PURPOSE FOR READING

Tell students they will read the selection and answer the questions that follow so they can get more practice using the reading strategies they have learned.

Possible Responses

Question 1

He was thinking about how his lungs were sick.

This student makes an inference based on story details. **Ask,** *What in the story makes you think so?*

the music

Think-along responses may be short. This is another appropriate inference based on story details. **Ask,** *What in the story makes you think so?*

2. What do you think made Derek feel so happy?

Derek got on the Internet and searched for a Web page with "Chris Brook" and "trumpet" on it. To his surprise, Mr. Brook had a Web page. On the page were pictures of the man and his trumpet. The site played clips of Chris Brook's music.

"Mom, come here! I want to show you something!" Derek yelled.

His mom came into the room. "What's so important?" she asked.

"I want you to hear this trumpet music. I heard this man play at school today. I want to learn to play a trumpet just like him," Derek said.

His mother looked sad. "I'm sorry, son. You can't play a trumpet," she said gently.

Derek frowned. "Why not?"

Mom sighed. "If you blew that hard, you would cough more. You already miss too much school."

Derek crossed his arms. "Dr. Allen always tells me to do breathing exercises. Wouldn't playing a trumpet be good exercise?"

Mom looked thoughtful. "You are going to see the doctor tomorrow. Why don't we ask him then?"

Derek nodded. "All right," he said.

3. What do you think the doctor will tell Derek?

111

Questions 2 and 3

He really liked the music.
This student's response shows attention to the main ideas and details of this text. **Ask,** *Why did this make him happy?*

He is feeling good.
This response draws from the text, but does not make it clear how or why he is feeling good. **Ask,** *What do you think is making him feel good?*

That he won't be able to play
This response is based on story details. Encourage this student to think critically about the text. **Ask,** *Why do you think so?*

I think the doctor will want him to do what makes him happy.
This student makes a prediction that may be based on experience. **Ask,** *What makes you think so?*

Derek wrote to Chris Brook at the e-mail address on his Web page.

```
Dear Mr. Brook,
I heard you play today. You were great! I want
to learn to play the trumpet, too. Your fan,
Derek Hunter
P.S. I was born with CF. CF stands for cystic
fibrosis. It makes my lungs sick. Do you know
anyone with CF who plays the trumpet?
```

After school the next day, Derek told the doctor that he wanted to play the trumpet. Dr. Allen shook his head.

"I know you want to do everything that other people do, but blowing a trumpet could hurt your lungs. Playing a trumpet takes a lot of air," the doctor said.

Derek sat up and tried to look his age. It wasn't easy when his feet hung down from the table.

"Dr. Allen, I have to play the trumpet," he said.

Now Dr. Allen looked unhappy. "Derek, if you use all that air blowing on a trumpet, it could make you cough more. Your lungs might get sick more often."

"I know how sick I am, Dr. Allen. That's why I have to try everything I can while I still feel like trying."

Dr. Allen sighed. "All right, Derek. I'm not going to stop you. But I will be keeping a close eye on you."

Derek slid down from the table and smiled.

> 4. Do you think Derek will learn to play the trumpet? Why do you think he will or will not?

Question 4

I think he won't because he can't with his breathing problems.

I think he will play because he really wants to and it would make him happy.

Both of these responses make reasonable predictions based on the story so far. Invite readers to continue reading to find out whether Derek will play the trumpet.

Derek went to the music store on Saturday. A woman helped him pick out a trumpet. It was brass, and it felt good in his hands. He tried to blow it, but no sound came out. After a few tries, he was able to blow a note.

"Do you know any trumpet teachers?" he asked.

"Just a minute." The woman looked in a book at her desk. She wrote down three names and telephone numbers. She handed the list to Derek.

A name on the list was Chris Brook!

"That's him. He's the man who played at the concert," Derek told his mom as they left the music store. "Can we call him?"

"Derek, you know he must be very busy." She opened the car door.

Derek hugged the trumpet case. "Thanks for the trumpet," he said.

His mother smiled. "Don't worry. We'll find a teacher."

After dinner, Derek tried to blow the trumpet again. He was starting to make a nice, clear sound. It made him cough a little but no more than he usually did.

Before he went to bed, he turned on the computer to check his e-mail. There was a message waiting for him from Chris Brook!

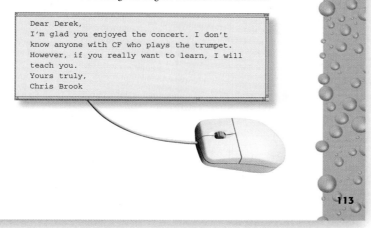

```
Dear Derek,
I'm glad you enjoyed the concert. I don't
know anyone with CF who plays the trumpet.
However, if you really want to learn, I will
teach you.
Yours truly,
Chris Brook
```

113

Notes

Explain that answering these questions will help students check their comprehension. Answering these questions will also help them practice for other reading tests.

Have students answer the questions. Explain that, as on other tests, each multiple-choice question has one right answer, but the last question can have more than one correct answer.

Answers to Theme Wrap-Up

1. **D. a boy who wants to play the trumpet even though he is sick.** (Inferential—Main Idea)

2. **D. The trumpet sounded strong and important.** (Inferential—Figurative Language)

3. **B. a musical sound.** (Inferential—Multiple-Meaning Words)

4. **A. He had never heard a prouder sound.** (Inferential—Fact/Opinion)

5. **C. He will e-mail Chris Brook to start his trumpet lessons.** (Inferential—Making Predictions)

6. Accept all reasonable responses, including: *He has a disease called cystic fibrosis and it makes it hard for him to breathe.* (Literal—Main Idea and Supporting Details)

CHOOSE A CHALLENGE *Wrap-Up*

➡ **Fill in the circle of the correct answer.**

1. This story is mostly about—
   Ⓐ famous trumpet players.
   Ⓑ a man who teaches his young friend how to play the trumpet.
   Ⓒ the disease of cystic fibrosis and how it makes people feel.
   Ⓓ a boy who wants to play the trumpet even though he is sick.

2. What do you think "he had never heard a prouder sound" means?
   Ⓐ The trumpet player stood tall.
   Ⓑ The trumpet sounded like a bell.
   Ⓒ The trumpet was loud.
   Ⓓ The trumpet sounded strong and important.

3. In this story, the word **note** means—
   Ⓐ a short letter or message.
   Ⓑ a musical sound.
   Ⓒ something important.
   Ⓓ a bad cough.

4. Which of the following is an opinion in this story?
   Ⓐ He had never heard a prouder sound.
   Ⓑ Back in class, Derek sat quietly.
   Ⓒ The teacher gave him a paper.
   Ⓓ There was a message waiting for him from Chris Brook!

5. What will Derek most likely do tomorrow when he wakes up?
   Ⓐ He will go to a music store to buy a new trumpet.
   Ⓑ He will decide that playing the trumpet is not a good idea.
   Ⓒ He will e-mail Chris Brook to start his trumpet lessons.
   Ⓓ He will go to school and sign up for the band.

6. Why are Derek's mother and his doctor worried about Derek playing the trumpet?

   _____

   _____

   _____

114

Notes

Henry B.

Henry B. Gonzalez was born in 1916 in San Antonio, Texas. Everyone called him "Henry B."

When Henry B. started first grade, he could not speak English, but only English was spoken at school. His parents were from Mexico, and only Spanish was spoken at home. School was very hard and scary for him. He could not answer questions the teacher asked because he did not understand her. He had to stay in first grade for two years. Henry B. did not like school.

> 1. Do you think Henry B. kept going to school? Explain what you think.

Henry B. had four brothers and one sister. Their parents wanted them to have a good education. Mr. and Mrs. Gonzalez talked about going home to Mexico, but schools were not as good. It was important for the Gonzalez children to learn as much as they could in San Antonio.

In those days, most of San Antonio's Mexican Americans lived in one part of the city. They could not go to some eating places. They couldn't use public parks or swimming pools. They could not drink from some water fountains.

115

PURPOSE FOR READING

Tell students they will read the selection and answer the questions that follow so they can get more practice using the reading strategies they have learned.

Question 1

I think he did because my parents say you have to.

This student connects the text with personal experience to make a prediction of what will happen next to Henry B.

He probably kept going to school or else we wouldn't be reading about him.

This student uses background knowledge to respond to this question. Encourage elaboration. **Ask,** *What makes you think so?*

Henry B. **discovered** the public library when he was eight years old. He soon learned to read in English. He loved to read, and he found that the more he read, the better he could read. Henry B. spent as many hours as he could in the library. First, he read cowboy stories. As he learned to understand the words, he read more difficult books.

When Mr. Gonzalez saw that Henry B. loved books, he began bringing books home from work. Mr. Gonzalez had gotten a job at a local newspaper. Henry B. loved history, the law, and books about people's lives. His father talked about the books with him. He also asked Henry B. to read books in English and Spanish. Sometimes Henry B. would copy some writing just because he liked the sound of the words.

2. How do you think Henry B.'s parents felt about his reading?

Henry B. did have one problem. People laughed at him when he spoke English. Henry B. did not like people making fun of him, so he decided to do something about it. He read that a great Greek teacher had learned to speak well by putting pebbles in his mouth and shouting into the sea breeze. Henry B. did not have a sea breeze, so he stood in front of a fan. Then he put marbles in his mouth and read aloud. His father told him to stop doing it because he could choke on a marble. Henry B. would not give up. He stood in front of the bathroom mirror and read aloud. His brothers and sisters hid under the bathroom window and laughed.

All of his work paid off. Henry B. was a very good middle-school and high-school student. He made good grades and played baseball. Later, he went to the University of Texas to study.

116

Question 2

They were happy. They wanted him to be educated.

This student connects story details to make an inference. Encourage this student to be more explicit. **Ask,** *Why do you think they wanted him to have a good education?*

proud

Responses to the Think-Along questions may be short. **Ask,** *What in the story makes you think so?*

3. What did Henry B. do when something was difficult for him?

Henry B. as a Young Man

Joaquin, Henry B.'s brother, also went to the University of Texas. Because they were Mexican Americans and poor, the two brothers had a hard time. They lived in a room with no heat. They slept under newspapers to keep warm.

The brothers could not get jobs near the university. They could not go into some eating places. Joaquin and Henry B. were given one meal a day for cleaning rooms in the rooming house where they lived. Henry B. did not eat enough good food, so he became ill. He returned to San Antonio where he could find work and go to law school.

Henry B. met Bertha Cuellar when he was 22 years old. He was very shy, and he joked to cover up his shyness. Both Henry B. and Bertha liked to read books. Bertha also liked to dance. She had many dance partners at parties. At one party, Bertha noticed that no one but Henry B. asked her to dance. Later she learned that Henry B. had told everyone that they were a couple. They weren't even dating! Henry B. and Bertha were married in 1940. Over their many years together, they had eight children.

Henry B. finished law school at St. Mary's University. He never worked as a lawyer. He wanted to run for office and help people. Henry B.'s parents did not think he should run for an office. Henry B. wanted to please his parents, but he saw this as a chance to make a difference in people's lives.

117

Question 3

He tried harder and didn't give up.

This response shows that the student is making connections between story details in order to make a statement about Henry B.'s character.

He felt bad.

This student may be focusing on the details on the first page of the story that told how difficult school was for Henry B. Encourage this student to think beyond these specific details. Say, *The story does say he felt bad when he was young. What else did he do when something was difficult?*

4. Is Henry B. someone you want to be like? Tell why you feel this way.

Henry B.'s Years of Service

In 1950 no one believed that a Mexican American could hold office. Henry B.'s friends told him he was crazy, but he would not listen. He ran for the city council, and he won. As a member of the city council, Henry B. led the fight to let Mexican Americans use San Antonio's city swimming pools. Next, he ran for the Texas Senate. Again, he won. He was the first Mexican American to hold a seat in the state senate in 110 years. As a Texas senator, Henry B. worked hard for Mexican Americans to have the same rights as others in Texas.

In 1961 Henry B. ran for a seat in the United States House of Representatives. Once again, Henry B. won. He was the first Mexican American from Texas in the House of Representatives. In Washington he fought hard for the rights of all people.

Henry B. died on November 28, 2000. He had served the 20th District of Texas for 38 years. Toward the end of his life, Henry B. said that serving his country was the greatest honor he could have had.

Question 4

I'd like to be like him because he works hard and wants to make a difference.

This response uses details from the selection to generate an opinion. **Ask,** *Why would you like to have these qualities?*

No, because he is too serious.

This student focuses on certain details from the selection to generate this response. **Ask,** *Does Henry B. have any qualities that you would like to have?*

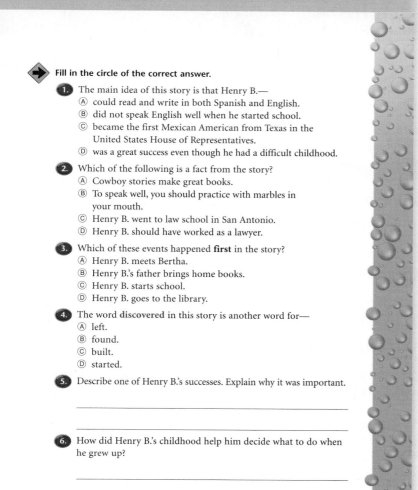

➤ **Fill in the circle of the correct answer.**

1. The main idea of this story is that Henry B.—
  Ⓐ could read and write in both Spanish and English.
  Ⓑ did not speak English well when he started school.
  Ⓒ became the first Mexican American from Texas in the United States House of Representatives.
  Ⓓ was a great success even though he had a difficult childhood.

2. Which of the following is a fact from the story?
  Ⓐ Cowboy stories make great books.
  Ⓑ To speak well, you should practice with marbles in your mouth.
  Ⓒ Henry B. went to law school in San Antonio.
  Ⓓ Henry B. should have worked as a lawyer.

3. Which of these events happened **first** in the story?
  Ⓐ Henry B. meets Bertha.
  Ⓑ Henry B.'s father brings home books.
  Ⓒ Henry B. starts school.
  Ⓓ Henry B. goes to the library.

4. The word **discovered** in this story is another word for—
  Ⓐ left.
  Ⓑ found.
  Ⓒ built.
  Ⓓ started.

5. Describe one of Henry B.'s successes. Explain why it was important.

_____

_____

6. How did Henry B.'s childhood help him decide what to do when he grew up?

_____

_____

119

Explain that answering these questions will help students check their comprehension. Answering these questions will also help them practice for other reading tests.

Have students answer the questions. Explain that, as on other tests, each multiple-choice question has one right answer, but the last two questions can have more than one correct answer.

Answers to Theme Wrap-Up

1. **D. was a great success even though he had a difficult childhood.** (Inferential—Main Idea)
2. **C. Henry B. went to law school in San Antonio.** (Inferential—Fact/Opinion)
3. **C. Henry B. starts school.** (Literal—Sequence)
4. **B. found.** (Inferential—Vocabulary)
5. Accept all reasonable responses, including: *It was important that he was the first Mexican American to be in politics because he set an example for other people.* (Inferential—Opinion)
6. Accept all reasonable responses, including: *He knew what it was like to be treated differently so he wanted to change that.* (Inferential—Cause-Effect)

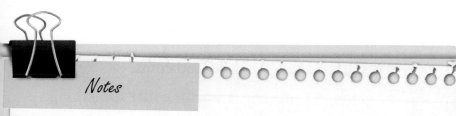

Notes

Glossary

amazing (uh MAYZ ihng) *adjective* Something that is surprising or wonderful is amazing.

arrested (uh REHST ehd) *adjective* Arrested means taken by the police for breaking the law.

assembly line (uh SEHM blee LYN) *noun* An assembly line is a moving belt like the ones you see at the store. The belt is used to move things. Each worker adds a different part to the thing.

auto (AWT oh) *adjective* Auto is another word for car. Auto is short for automobile.

awesome (AW suhm) *adjective* Awesome means amazing.

basis (BAY sihs) *noun* A basis means a beginning point.

beg (BEHG) *verb* To beg means to ask for something.

blond (BLAHND) *adjective* Blond is a hair color that is very light.

booth (BOOTH) *noun* A booth is a small building at a fair where you can play a game or buy food.

carnival (KAHR nuh vuhl) *noun* A carnival is a fair with games, rides, and food.

cash (KASH) *adjective* Cash is money in bills and coins.

caution (KAW shuhn) *noun* A caution is a warning that something is not safe.

choices (CHOYS uhz) *noun* Choices are things that you choose between.

claimed (KLAYMD) *verb* Claimed means said something that you believed was true or wanted others to believe.

comb (KOHM) *noun* A comb is a tool used for brushing hair.

comeback (KUHM bak) *noun* A comeback happens when a person or thing that used to be popular becomes popular again.

community service (kuh MYOO nuh tee SUR vihs) *noun*
Community service is work that helps someone. People who have broken the law sometimes do this work. They do not get paid.

concrete (KAHN kreet) *adjective* Something that is concrete is made of a hard mix of sand, clay, and water.

construction area (kuhn STRUHK shuhn EHR ee uh) *noun*
A construction area is a place where a building is being made.

continent (KAHNT ihn uhnt) *noun* A continent is a very large piece of land on Earth.

crew (KROO) *noun* A crew is the people who work on a ship.

curved (KURVD) *verb* Curved means rounded or bent like part of a circle.

demanded (dee MAND ehd) *verb* Demanded means asked for something but not in a nice way.

demonstrated (DEHM uhn strayt ehd) *verb* To have demonstrated something means to have shown someone how to do it.

difference (DIHF uhr uhns) *noun* Difference is the way in which things are not alike.

disappeared (dihs uh PIHRD) *verb* Disappeared means went out of sight.

drawers (DRAW uhrz) *noun* Drawers are boxes in a dresser that can be pulled out. They are used to keep clothes in.

examined (ehg ZAM uhnd) *verb* Examined means looked at something very carefully.

explore (ehk SPLAWR) *verb* To explore is to travel to and learn about new lands.

explorer (ehk SPLAWR uhr) *noun* An explorer is a person who travels to and learns about new lands.

features (FEE chuhrz) *noun* Features are special parts of a thing, such as the door or color of a car.

headlights (HEHD lyts) *noun* Headlights are the front lights of a car that light up the road at night.

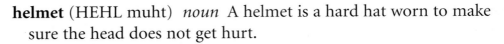

helmet (HEHL muht) *noun* A helmet is a hard hat worn to make sure the head does not get hurt.

hoax (HOHKS) *noun* A hoax is a trick or mean joke.

hoops (HOOPS) *noun* Hoops are large rings or circles that are sometimes made of plastic.

icebergs (YS burgz) *noun* Icebergs are huge chunks of ice that float in cold seas.

improve (ihm PROOV) *verb* To improve means to make something better than it was before.

industry (IHN duhs tree) *noun* An industry is a group that makes something to sell.

interrupted (ihn tuh RUHPT ehd) *verb* To have interrupted someone means to have spoken while he or she was doing something else.

invented (ihn VEHN tehd) *adjective* Something that has been invented has been thought about and then made for the first time.

inventors (ihn VEHN tuhrz) *noun* Inventors are people who think of new ideas and make new things.

jail (JAYL) *noun* A jail is a building for people who have broken the law.

journals (JUR nuhlz) *noun* Journals are blank books that people write their thoughts in.

judge (JUHJ) *noun* A judge decides if someone should go to jail.

killer whales (KIHL uhr WAYLZ) *noun* Killer whales are large black and white animals that live in the ocean and eat fish and seals.

laws (LAWZ) *noun* Laws are rules made by a city, state, or country. Laws tell you what you can and cannot do.

magazine (MAG uh zeen) *noun* A magazine is a paper booklet that has stories and pictures in it.

metal (MEHT l) *adjective* Metal means made of iron or another shiny solid, such as silver.

model (MAHD l) *adjective* Model means a smaller form of something.

motor (MOHT uhr) *noun* A motor is a machine that makes something move.

neat (NEET) *adjective* Neat means clean.

nonstop (NAHN STAHP) *adjective* Something that is nonstop keeps going without a stop.

opinions (uh PIHN yuhnz) *noun* Opinions are what people think or believe about something.

owes (OHZ) *verb* Someone who owes something has to pay it back.

pain (PAYN) *noun* A pain is someone who makes other people angry.

performed (puhr FAWRMD) *adjective* To be performed means to be put on, as in an act or show.

plastic (PLAS tihk) *noun* Plastic is a solid used to make strong objects.

posters (POHS tuhrz) *noun* Posters are big pieces of paper covered by pictures and words.

purse (PURS) *noun* A purse is a small bag for carrying money and other things.

quarter (KWAWRT uhr) *noun* A quarter is a coin that is worth 25 cents.

ramps (RAMPS) *noun* Ramps are flat places that are raised at one end.

receipt (rih SEET) *noun* A receipt is a piece of paper that you get when you buy something.

reminded (rih MYND ehd) *verb* Reminded means helped someone remember something.

rumor (ROO muhr) *noun* A rumor is a story told as news and passed from person to person. A rumor may or may not be true.

seals (SEELZ) *noun* Seals are animals with smooth skins that live in cold oceans.

searched (SURCHD) *verb* Searched means looked for someone or something.

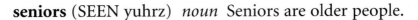

seniors (SEEN yuhrz) *noun* Seniors are older people.

sentence (SEHNT ns) *verb* To sentence means to make someone who broke the law spend time in jail or do some work.

sideshows (SYD shohz) *noun* Sideshows are circus shows that are not in the main tent.

skateboard (SKAYT bawrd) *noun* A skateboard is a short board with wheels at both ends.

skaters (SKAYT uhrz) *noun* Skaters are people who ride skateboards.

stole (STOHL) *verb* Stole means took something without asking.

suitcase (SOOT kays) *noun* A suitcase is a box to put clothes in. It is used when traveling.

supplies (suh PLYZ) *noun* Supplies are things you need for a job or trip.

surfers (SURF uhrz) *noun* Surfers are people who ride ocean waves on surfboards.

swamp (SWAHMP) *noun* A swamp is a piece of wet land that is full of mud, water, and plants.

thrill (THRIHL) *noun* A thrill is something that makes a person have a strange or happy feeling.

tickets (TIHK ihts) *noun* Tickets are pieces of paper that you buy to be allowed to do something.

vehicles (VEE uh kuhlz) *noun* Vehicles are things that people drive or ride in.

wheelchairs (WEEL chehrz) *noun* Wheelchairs are chairs on wheels. These chairs are used by people who cannot walk.